Best
Garden Plants
for
Georgia

Tara Dillard
Don Williamson

Lone Pine Publishing International

© 2006 by Lone Pine Publishing International Inc.
First printed in 2006   10 9 8 7 6 5 4 3 2 1
Printed in China

The Distributor: Lone Pine Publishing
1808 B Street NW, Suite 140
Auburn, WA, USA 98001
Website: www.lonepinepublishing.com

Library and Archives Canada Cataloguing in Publication
Dillard, Tara
    Best garden plants for Georgia / Tara Dillard, Don Williamson.

Includes index.
ISBN–13: 978-976-8200-09-9
ISBN–10: 976-8200-09-X

    1. Plants, Ornamental—Georgia. 2. Gardening—Georgia.
I. Williamson, Don, 1962– II. Title.

SB453.2.G4D45 2006   635.9'09758   C2005–906886–8

Scanning & Electronic Film: Elite Lithographers Co.

Front cover photographs by Tim Matheson and Tamara Eder except where noted. *Clockwise from top right:* Marchesa Boccella rose, flowering cherry, cosmos, sassafras (Laura Peters), daylily, grancy gray-beard, daylily (Allison Penko), lily (Laura Peters), coreopsis, lily (Erika Flatt).

Photography: All photos by Tim Matheson, Tamara Eder and Laura Peters, except: Pam Beck 79b, 81b, 101a, 170a&b; Callaway Gardens (Stone Mountain, GA) 65a; David Cavagnaro 27b; Derek Fell 27a, 28a, 32a, 39a, 46a, 52a&b, 55a&b, 61a&b, 68a&b, 72a&b, 78a, 97a&b, 100a, 103a&b, 104a, 111a, 114, 124a, 131, 132a&b, 136a&b, 142, 143b, 145a, 146a, 147b, 160a, 164b; Erika Flatt 144a; Anne Gordon 14a, 28b; Chris Hansen-Terra Nova Nurseries 65b; Lynne Harrison 79a; Richard Hawke-CBG 42b; Saxon Holt 78b, 104b, 111b, 113a, 145b, 160b, 164a, 168; Horticolor (N0900738) 57b; Jackson & Perkins 110a; Liz Klose 167a; Debra Knapke 125a; Dawn Loewen 60a,106a&b; Janet Loughrey 120a, 146b, 159b; Marilynn McAra 139b; Kim O'Leary 15a, 19a, 21a&b, 43a&b, 59a, 76a, 87b, 94a&b, 153b; Allison Penko 24b, 40a, 53a, 63a&b, 69a&b, 75a&b, 95b, 99b, 122a, 123b, 130a, 137b, 148b, 158a, 163b, 166a, 167b, 169a; Photos.com 139a, 143a; Robert Ritchie 38b, 46b, 50a&b, 56a&b, 85a&b, 98a, 115a; Peter Thompstone 49b; Mark Turner 71a, 80a&b, 120b, 124b, 140a&b, 147a; Don Williamson 141a&b, 150a; Tim Wood 133a.

Table of Contents

Introduction

Starting a garden can seem like a daunting task. Which plants should you choose? Where in the garden should you put them? This book is intended to give beginning gardeners the information they need to start planning and planting gardens of their own. It describes a wide variety of plants and provides basic planting information, such as where and how to plant.

Georgia encompasses a wide diversity of ecological regions, and each presents its own unique challenges. Each region has a temperature range that indicates relative hardiness. Consider this: 5° F for a plant is very different with snow cover or without, in soggy soil or in dry soil, and following a hot summer or a long, cold, wet one. Such factors are at least as important to plant survival as is temperature.

Hardiness zones and frost dates are two concepts often used when discussing climate. Hardiness zones are based on the average low temperatures and conditions in winter. Plants are rated based on the hardiness zones in which they can grow successfully. The average last-frost date in spring combined with the average first-frost date in fall allows us to predict the length of the growing season. Recognizing the type of climate where you garden helps determine which plants you can expect to survive winter. Your local garden center and county extension agent can provide you with local hardiness zones and frost date information.

Getting Started

When planning your garden, start with a quick analysis of the garden as it is now. Plants have varied requirements, and it is easier to put the right plant in the right place than to change your garden to suit the plants you want.

Knowing which parts of your garden receive the most and least amounts of sunlight helps you choose the appropriate plants for these locations. The amount of sun a site receives is generally described with the following terms: full sun (direct, unobstructed light for all or most of the day); partial shade (direct sun for about half the day and shade for the rest); light shade (shade for all or for most of the day, with some sun filtering through to ground level); and full shade (no direct sunlight). Most plants prefer a specific amount of light, but many can adapt to a range of light levels.

Plants use soil to hold themselves upright, but they also rely on the many resources it holds: air, water, nutrients, organic matter and a host of microbes. The particle size of the soil influences the amount of air, water and nutrients it can hold. Sand, with the largest particles, has a lot of air space and allows water and nutrients to drain quickly. Clay, with the smallest particles, is high in nutrients but has very little air space. Water is

therefore slow to penetrate clay and slow to drain from it.

Soil acidity or alkalinity (measured on the pH scale) influences the nutrients available to plants. A pH of 7 is neutral; a lower pH is more acidic. Most plants prefer a soil with a pH of 5.5–7.5. Soil-testing kits are available at most garden centers, and soil samples can be sent to your county extension office for a more thorough analysis.

Compost is one of the best and most important amendments you can add to any type of soil. Compost improves soil by adding organic matter and nutrients, introducing soil microbes, increasing water retention and improving drainage. Compost can be purchased, or you can make it in your own backyard.

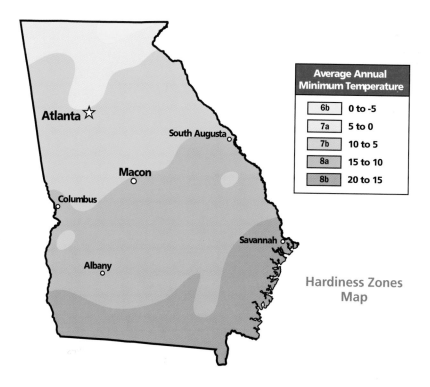

Hardiness Zones Map

Microclimates are small areas that are generally warmer or colder than the surrounding area. Buildings, fences, trees and other large objects can provide extra shelter in winter, and they may trap heat in summer, thereby creating a warmer microclimate. The bottoms of hills are usually colder than the tops, but are often less windy. Take advantage of these special areas when you plan your garden and choose your plants. In a warm, sheltered location, you may be able to successfully grow out-of-zone plants.

Selecting Plants

It's important to purchase healthy plants that are free of pests and diseases. Such plants establish quickly and won't introduce problems that may spread to other plants. You should have a good idea of what the plant is supposed to look like—its growth habit and the color and shape of the leaves—and then inspect the plant for signs of disease or pest infestation.

Most plants for sale are container grown. Containers are an efficient way for nurseries and greenhouses to grow plants, but a plant grown in a restricted space for too long can become pot bound, with its roots densely encircling the inside of the pot. Avoid purchasing root-bound plants, because they are often stressed and can take longer to establish or may not establish at all. You can often temporarily remove the pot to examine the roots. At the same time, check for soil-borne insects and rotten roots. Healthy roots are white to light brown in color.

Planting Basics

The following tips apply to all plants:

- Know the mature size. Place your plants based on their size at maturity rather than how big they are when you plant them. Large plants should have enough room to mature without interfering with walls, roof overhangs, power lines and walkways.

- Prepare the garden before planting. Dig over the soil, pull up any weeds and make any needed amendments before you begin planting, if possible. These preparations may be more difficult in established beds to which you want to add a single plant. The prepared area should be at least twice the size of the plant you want to put in, and preferably the expected size of the mature plant's root system.

- Accommodate the rootball. If you prepared your planting spot ahead of time, your planting hole needs to be only big enough to accommodate the root ball with the roots spread out slightly.

- Unwrap the roots. To allow the roots to spread out naturally, it is always best to remove any container before planting. In particular, you should remove plastic containers, fiber pots, wire and burlap before planting trees. Fiber pots

Gently remove container.

Ensure proper planting depth.

Backfill with soil.

decompose very slowly, if at all, and wick moisture away from the plant. Synthetic burlap won't decompose, and wire can strangle the roots as they mature. The only exceptions to this rule are peat pots and pellets used to start annuals and vegetables; they decompose and can be planted with the young transplants.

- Plant at the same depth in the soil. Plants generally like to grow at a specific level in relation to the soil and should be planted at the same level they were growing at before you transplanted them.

- Settle the soil with water. Good contact between the roots and the soil is important, but pressing the soil down too firmly, as often happens when you step on it, can cause compaction. This reduces the movement of water through the soil and leaves very few air spaces. Instead, pour water in as you fill the hole with soil. The water will settle the soil evenly without allowing it to compact.

- Identify your plants. Keep track of what's what by putting a tag next to each plant when you plant it or recording plant names and locations on a bird's-eye sketch map of your garden. Over time, it is very easy to forget exactly what you planted and where.

- Water deeply and infrequently. It's better to water deeply once every week or two than to water lightly more frequently. Deep watering forces roots to grow as they search for water and helps the plants survive dry spells when water bans may restrict your watering regime. Always check the root zone before you water. More gardeners overwater than underwater.

Annuals

Annuals are expected to last only for a single growing season. Their flowers and decorative foliage provide bright splashes of color and can fill in spaces around immature trees, shrubs and perennials.

Annuals are easy to plant and are usually sold in small packs of four or six. The roots quickly fill the space in these small packs, so the small rootball should be broken up before planting. Split the ball in two up the center or run your thumb up each side to break up the roots.

Many annuals are grown from seed. Plants that dislike their roots being disturbed do best when sown in place or grown in peat pots or pellets to minimize root disturbance.

Winter annuals can be planted in late fall and early winter. Summer annuals can be planted in spring. Be aware of your local frost dates, because some summer annuals are quite tender.

Settle backfilled soil with water.

Water the plant well.

Add a layer of mulch.

Perennials

Perennials grow for three or more years. They usually die back to the ground each fall and send up new shoots in spring, although some are evergreen. They often have a shorter period of bloom than annuals but require less care.

Many perennials benefit from being divided every few years. Doing so keeps them growing and blooming vigorously and is often helpful in controlling their spread. Dividing involves digging the plant up, removing dead bits, breaking or cutting the plant into several pieces and replanting some or all of them. Extra pieces can become gifts for family, friends and neighbors.

Trees & Shrubs

Trees and shrubs provide the bones of the garden. They are often the slowest growing plants but usually the longest lived. They may be characterized by deciduous or evergreen leaf type, or broad-leaved or needled.

Trees should have as little disturbed soil as possible at the bottom of the planting hole. Loose dirt settles over time, and sinking even an inch can kill some trees.

Roses are lovely on their own or in mixed borders.

Staking, sometimes recommended for newly planted trees, is necessary only for trees over 5' tall.

Pruning is more often required for shrubs than trees. It helps them maintain an attractive shape and can improve blooming. If you have never pruned before, it is a good idea to take a pruning course or to hire or consult with an ISA (International Society of Arboriculture) certified arborist.

Roses

Roses are beautiful shrubs with lovely, often-fragrant blooms. Traditionally, most roses bloomed only once per year, but most new varieties bloom for much or all of summer.

Generally, roses prefer a fertile, well-prepared planting area, although many roses are quite durable and adapt to poorer conditions. As a guide, prepare a circular area 24" in diameter and 24" deep. Add plenty of compost or other fertile organic matter. Keep roses well watered during the growing season (approximately 1" of water per week). Like all shrubs, roses have specific pruning requirements.

Trees and shrubs provide backbone to the mixed border.

Training vines to climb arbors adds structure to the garden.

Lilies bloom throughout the summer.

Bulbs, Corms & Tubers

Some plants have fleshy underground storage organs that allow them to survive extended periods of dormancy. They are often grown for the bright splashes of color their flowers provide. They may flower in spring, summer or fall.

Hardy selections can be left in the ground to flower every year. The bulbs, corms or tubers of tender plants are generally lifted from the garden as the foliage dies back in fall, then stored in a cool, frost-free location until being replanted in spring.

Herbs

Herbs may be medicinal, culinary or both. A few common culinary herbs are listed in this book. Even if you don't cook with them, the often-fragrant foliage adds its aroma to the garden, and the plants have decorative forms, leaves and flowers.

Many herbs have flowers that attract butterflies, bees and hummingbirds. They also attract predatory insects, which help to manage pest problems by feasting on problem insects such as aphids, mealy bugs and whiteflies.

Vines & Groundcovers

Vines or climbing plants are useful for screening and shade, especially where a tree won't fit. They may be woody or herbaceous and annual or perennial.

Most vines need sturdy support, such as a trellis, arbor, porch railing, fence, wall, pole or tree. To avoid disturbing the vine's roots, install any necessary supports before planting.

Pretty well any plant that covers the ground can be used as a groundcover. Groundcovers are often spreading plants with dense growth that are used to control soil erosion, keep weeds at bay and fill garden areas that are difficult to maintain.

Groundcovers can be herbaceous or woody and annual or perennial. Aggressive vines make excellent groundcovers, but any densely growing plant that covers the ground can be used. Small plants or ones with a slow spread need to be placed close enough together to be effective.

Herbs are attractive and useful garden plants.

Ferns & Ornamental Grasses

Consider foliage when choosing plants for your garden. Although spectacular in bloom, many plants can seem rather dull without flowers. Include in your garden a variety of plants with unique, interesting or striking foliage to provide all the color and texture you want without the need to rely on flowers.

Ferns and ornamental grasses are two main groups of foliage plants. In addition, we have included throughout the book a variety of annuals, perennials, trees, shrubs, vines and herbs with wonderful foliage that will be assets to your garden landscape.

Ornamental grasses add color, variety and texture.

Ferns are ancient plants that have adapted to many different environments. This large group of plants offers interesting foliage in a wide array of shapes and colors. Instead of producing flowers, ferns reproduce by spores borne in structures on the undersides and margins of the foliage. Ferns are generally planted in moist, shaded gardens, but some will thrive in dry shade under the deep shade of some trees, such as oak and magnolia.

Ornamental grasses are becoming very popular garden additions. They offer a variety of textures and foliage colors, providing at least three seasons of interest. There is an ornamental grass for every garden situation and condition, from hot and dry to cool and wet, and any type of soil.

Ornamental grasses have few insect or disease problems. Other than cutting back perennial species in fall or spring, little maintenance is required. Be aware that dried grass is highly flammable. Left standing for winter interest, it can be a fire hazard, so cut back grasses near houses and other structures in fall.

Final Comments

We encourage you to visit the outstanding garden shows, county fairs, public gardens, garden tours, arboretums and private gardens (get permission first) we have here in Georgia to see which plants grow best and which ones catch your interest. A walk through your neighborhood is also a grand way to see which plants might do well in your own garden. Don't be afraid to ask questions.

Also, don't be afraid to experiment. No matter how many books you read, trying things yourself is the best way to learn and to find out what will grow in your garden. Use the information provided as guidelines, and have fun!

Begonia
Begonia

B. *rex-cultorum* 'Escargot' (above), B. x *tuberhybrida* (below)

Whether you want beautiful flowers, a compact habit or decorative foliage, there is a begonia to fulfill your gardening needs.

Growing
Wax begonias with bronze or reddish foliage prefer **full sun** or **partial shade,** whereas those with green or variegated leaves prefer **partial to full shade.** Tuberous and rex begonias prefer **light or partial shade.** The soil should be **fertile, neutral to acidic** and **well drained,** with a lot of **organic matter**.

Allow the soil to dry out slightly between waterings, particularly for tuberous begonias. Plant begonias only in warm soil; in cold soil, they may become stunted and fail to thrive.

Tips
Plant trailing tuberous begonias in hanging baskets and containers. Wax begonias make attractive large drifts and edging plants. Rex begonias are useful as specimen plants in containers and beds.

Recommended
Over 1300 begonia species exist, along with a plethora of cultivars.

B. rex-cultorum (rex begonias) are grown for their dramatic colorful foliage.

B. semperflorens-cultorum (wax begonias) have a neat, rounded habit, with pink, white, red or bicolored flowers and green, bronze, reddish or white-variegated foliage.

B. x tuberhybrida (tuberous begonias), generally sold as tubers, bear flowers in many shades of red, pink, yellow, orange or white.

Features: pink, white, red, yellow, orange, bicolored or picotee flowers; decorative foliage
Height: 6–24" **Spread:** 6–24"

Calendula
Calendula

Bright and charming, calendula produces attractive flowers in warm colors in late winter and spring.

Growing

Calendula does well in **full sun,** in **well-drained** soil of **average fertility.** It likes cool weather and can withstand a light frost. Deadhead to prolong blooming and keep the plants looking neat.

Young plants are sometimes difficult to find in nurseries. Sow seed directly into the garden in mid-fall. A second sowing in early winter ensures a good spring display.

Tips

This informal plant looks attractive in borders and in mixed planters. Cold-hardy calendula often continues flowering through late winter storms and frosts.

Recommended

C. officinalis is a vigorous, tough, upright plant that bears daisy-like, single or double flowers in a wide range of yellow and orange shades. Several cultivars are available.

C. officinalis 'Apricot Surprise' (above)
C. officinalis (below)

Calendula flowers are popular kitchen herbs that can be added to stews for color or to salads for flavor. They can also be brewed into an infusion that is useful as a wash for minor cuts and bruises.

Also called: pot marigold, English marigold
Features: cream, yellow, gold, orange or apricot flowers; long blooming period
Height: 12–30" **Spread:** 12–18"

Coleus

Solenostemon (Coleus)

There is a coleus for everyone. This plant has almost limitless colors, textures and variations.

Growing

Coleus prefers **light shade** or **partial shade** but tolerates full shade that isn't too dense and full sun if the plants are watered regularly. The soil should be **average to fertile, humus rich, moist** and **well drained**.

Place the seeds in a refrigerator for one or two days before planting them on the soil surface. They need light to germinate. Green at first, the seedlings develop leaf variegation as they mature.

Tips

Coleus looks dramatic when grouped in beds, borders and mixed containers or planted as edging.

Coleus tends to stretch out and become less attractive after flowering. Simply pinch off the developing flower buds.

Recommended

S. scutellarioides (*Coleus blumei* var. *verschaffeltii*) forms a bushy mound of multi-colored, slightly toothed to very ruffled foliage. Many cultivars are available, but some cannot be started from seed. Recent introductions that tolerate full sun and have larger, more colorful foliage are available.

S. *scutellarioides* cultivar (above)
S. *scutellarioides* mixed cultivars (below)

Try taking coleus cuttings from a mother plant and overwintering them inside. The cuttings root easily in a glass of water.

Features: brightly colored foliage
Height: 6–36" **Spread:** usually equal to height

Cosmos

Cosmos

C. sulphureus 'Sunny Red' (above), C. sulphureus (below)

Cosmos is a low-cost, low-maintenance, cottage-garden flower that is easy to grow and never fails to delight. It can handle the toughest, driest conditions we have in the Peach State.

Growing

Cosmos likes **full sun** and soil of **average fertility** that is **well drained**. Overfertilizing and overwatering can reduce the number of flowers. Deadhead to encourage more flowers. Plant out transplants or direct sow the seeds into warm soil after the last frost. Cosmos often self-seeds.

Tips

Cosmos look attractive in cottage gardens, in borders or mass planted in informal beds. A second sowing in mid-summer provides a colorful fall show.

Recommended

C. sulphureus (yellow cosmos) is an erect, dense plant that bears gold, orange, scarlet or yellow flowers.

The name cosmos is from the Greek kosmos, *meaning 'good order' or 'harmony.'*

Features: gold, orange, scarlet or yellow flowers; attractive foliage; easy to grow
Height: 12–36" **Spread:** 12–24"

Dusty Miller

Senecio

S. *cineraria* 'Cirrus' (above), S. *cineraria* (below)

Dusty miller is a great addition to planters, window boxes and mixed borders where the deeply lobed, soft, silvery gray foliage makes a good backdrop for the brightly colored flowers of other annuals.

Growing

Dusty miller grows well in **full sun** or **partial shade**. The soil should be of **average fertility** and **well drained**.

Tips

The soft, lacy, silvery foliage of this plant is its main feature. Dusty miller is used primarily as an edging plant but also in beds, borders and containers.

Pinch off the flowers before they bloom. They aren't showy, and they use energy that would otherwise go to producing more foliage.

Features: silvery foliage; neat habit; yellow to cream flowers **Height:** 12–24" **Spread:** equal to height or slightly narrower

Dusty miller is a subshrub that we use as an annual.

Recommended

S. cineraria forms a mound of fuzzy, silvery gray foliage that is lobed or finely divided. Many cultivars with impressive foliage shades and shapes have been developed.

A wonderful filler for fresh- or dried-flower arrangements, dusty miller adds a lacy texture.

English Daisy

Bellis

B. perennis (above), *B. perennis* cultivar (below)

nglish daisy works well with spring-blooming bulbs. It is at its best in cool weather and can sulk during the hot summer.

Growing

English daisy grows well in **full sun, partial shade** or **light shade**. The soil should be of **average to high fertility, humus rich, cool** and **moist**.

Tips

Use English daisy on rock walls, in open woodland gardens, in planters, to edge borders and as a groundcover.

English daisy has the habit of self-seeding and is prone to show up where you least expect it, including lawns. Deadheading controls this tendency but, if immaculate lawns are desired, place this species well away from them.

Recommended

B. perennis is a low, spreading perennial that is best used as an annual or biennial. The white, pink or red flowers have yellow centers. **Habanera Series** has flowers with similar colors, but with long petals. **'Pomponette'** also has flowers in these colors, but with 'quilled' petals (rolled into tubes lengthways). **'White Carpet'** has white, double flowers.

Features: yellow-centered, white, pink or red early-spring flowers **Height:** 2–8" **Spread:** 2–8"

Foxglove
Digitalis

Foxglove happily self-seeds and often pops up in new combinations with other plants.

Growing

Foxglove grows well in **partial or light shade,** in **fertile, humus-rich, moist** soil. It adapts to most soils that are neither too wet nor too dry. Plants in windy locations may need staking.

If you allow a few flower spikes to produce seeds, foxglove will self-seed and continue to inhabit your garden. Extra seedlings can be thinned out or transplanted to a new location—perhaps a friend's garden.

Tips

Foxglove is a biennial that we grow as an annual. Sow seed directly, plant cell packs in fall or purchase one-gallon plants in spring. Foxglove makes an excellent vertical accent along the middle to back of a border and is an interesting addition to woodland gardens with filtered light.

Recommended

D. purpurea forms a basal rosette of foliage from which tall flowering spikes in a wide range of colors emerge. **Excelsior Hybrids** bear dense spikes of flowers. **Foxy Hybrids** are considered dwarf by foxglove standards.

D. purpurea (above & below)

Pause to look up inside a tubular foxglove flower and discover the contrasting freckles and spots that decorate it.

Features: attractive spring to early-summer flowers in pink, purple, yellow, maroon, red or white; attractive habit **Height:** 2–5'
Spread: 24"

Geranium

Pelargonium

P. peltatum cultivar (above & below)

Geraniums have earned their respected place in the annual garden, but be sure to buy plants that can take Georgia's heat and humidity.

Growing

Zonal and scented geraniums perform best in **full sun,** but regal and ivy-leaved geraniums prefer **partial shade.** The soil should be **fertile** and **well drained.** Deadheading, by hand and not with pruners, is essential to keep geraniums blooming and looking neat. Geraniums can be damaged by heavy rains.

Tips

Geraniums are popular for use in borders, beds, planters, hanging baskets and window boxes. Regal and scented geraniums should not be used in beds or borders.

Recommended

P. x *domesticum* (regal geranium, Martha Washington geranium) has heart-shaped leaves and larger, frillier flowers than other geraniums. It works best in containers; it tends not to perform well planted directly in the ground. This plant does not tolerate heat as well as other varieties do.

P. x *hortorum* (zonal geranium) is a bushy plant with red, pink, purple, orange or white flowers. The leaves are frequently banded or multi-colored.

P. peltatum (ivy-leaved geranium) has thick, waxy leaves and a trailing habit. It is one of the best plants to include in a mixed hanging basket.

P. **species** and **cultivars** (scented geraniums) have fragrant and often-decorative foliage. The scents are grouped into the categories of rose, mint, citrus, fruit, spice and pungent.

Features: red, pink, violet, orange, salmon, white or purple flowers; decorative or scented foliage; variable habit **Height:** 8–24"
Spread: 6"–4'

Globe Amaranth

Gomphrena

Globe amaranths are wonderful annuals for our hot summers. With the range in flower colors and plant sizes, there is a globe amaranth for every sunny, well-drained spot. Butterflies adore these plants.

Growing

Globe amaranths prefer **full sun,** in soil of **average fertility** that is **well drained**. Provide adequate moisture when the plants are young. Although established plants do tolerate drought and heat, they appreciate water during periods of extended drought. Deadhead to keep the plants tidy.

Soak the seeds in water for two to four days to encourage sprouting before sowing into warm soil (above 70° F). Seed sown in mid-summer produces a colorful fall show.

Tips

Globe amaranth can be included in informal and cottage gardens as well as mixed beds and borders.

Globe amaranth flowers are popular for cutting and drying. Harvest the blooms when they become round and plump; dry them upside down in a cool, dry location.

Recommended

G. globosa forms a rounded, bushy plant that bears papery, clover-like flowers in shades of purple, magenta, white or pink. Many cultivars are available, including especially compact selections.

G. **'Strawberry Fields'** is a hybrid plant that bears bright red flowers.

G. globosa (above & below)

The flowerheads of globe amaranths consist of brightly colored, papery bracts from which the tiny flowers emerge. Cut the blooms before the first frost for indoor dried flowers all winter.

Features: purple, magenta, pink, white or red flowers; easy to grow; tough as nails
Height: 6–30"   **Spread:** 6–15"

Impatiens

Impatiens

I. walleriana (above), *I. hawkeri* (below)

Impatiens are a staple of the shade garden. No other plants deliver masses of colorful flowers the way impatiens do in the shade.

Growing

I. balsamina and *I. walleriana* do best in **partial shade** or **light shade**, and *I. hawkeri* prefers **full sun**; in full shade, all three may get a little leggy. The soil should be **fertile, humus rich, moist** and **well drained**.

Tips

Impatiens are known for their ability to grow and flower profusely even in shade. Mass plant them in beds under trees,

Because I. walleriana *flowers continuously throughout the growing season, the British named it busy Lizzie.*

along shady fences or walls, or in porch planters. They also look lovely in hanging baskets.

Recommended

Many wonderful species of impatiens are available. The following are the most popular.

I. balsamina (balsam impatiens) is an upright plant that blooms in shades of purple, red, pink or white. Several cultivars have double flowers.

I. hawkeri (New Guinea impatiens) flowers in shades of red, orange, pink, purple or white. The foliage is often variegated with a yellow stripe down the center of each leaf.

I. walleriana (busy Lizzie) flowers in shades of purple, red, burgundy, pink, yellow, salmon, orange, apricot or white and can be bicolored. Many cultivars are available.

Features: bright flowers in shades of purple, red, burgundy, pink, yellow, salmon, orange, apricot, white or bicolored; grows well in shade **Height:** 6–36" **Spread:** 12–24"

Lantana
Lantana

*L*antanas that feature clusters of tiny orange and red flowers combine magically in pots with many heat-tolerant blue-flowered plants, such as salvia, ageratum, browallia and lobelia.

Growing

Lantana grows best in **full sun**. The soil should be **average to fertile, moist** and **well drained**. Lantana tolerates heat and drought. Without **good air circulation,** lantana can be prone to whiteflies. Lantana survives warm winters, but cuttings can also be taken in late summer and grown indoors through winter to supply next year's plants.

Tips

Lantana is a tender shrub that is grown as an annual. It makes an attractive addition to beds and borders as well as in mixed containers and hanging baskets. It is also a butterfly magnet.

Recommended

L. camara is a bushy plant that bears round clusters of flowers in a variety of colors. The flowers often change color as they mature, giving the flower clusters a striking, multi-colored appearance. 'Miss Huff' is a large, vigorous selection with orange and yellow flowers. It can act like a perennial in zone 7. **Patriot Series** plants flower in a wide range of colors and have minty, dark to medium green foliage.

L. camara cultivar (above & below)

Lantana is not intimidated by hot, dry weather, and a 3" bedding plant can reach the size of a small shrub in a single season.

Also called: shrub verbena **Features:** stunning flowers in combinations of yellow, orange, pink, purple, red or white; easy to grow; low maintenance **Height:** 1–5' **Spread:** 1–4'

Lisianthus

Eustoma

E. grandiflorum (above & below)

The true blue varieties of lisianthus are stunning when paired with bright yellow heat-loving flowers.

Growing

Lisianthus prefers **full sun,** but in hot weather it benefits from **protection** from the afternoon sun. The soil should be of **average fertility, neutral to alkaline** and **well drained.** Lisianthus can be damaged by heavy summer rainfall.

This plant can be quite slow to establish when sown directly in the garden. It is best to either start treated seed from reputable sources very early indoors in a location with good light, or purchase young transplants at the garden center. Dispose of any plants that appear to be diseased before the disease has a chance to spread to other plants.

Tips

All varieties of lisianthus look best grouped together in flowerbeds or containers. The tallest varieties, with their long-lasting blooms, are popular in cut-flower gardens. Children enjoy popping the thumb-sized buds.

Recommended

E. grandiflorum forms a slender, upright plant topped by satiny, cup-shaped flowers. **Echo Series** offers tall plants with double flowers in many colors. **Lisa Series** offers dwarf plants that bloom in many colors.

A small vase filled with satin-textured lisianthus flowers adds a touch of elegance to any table.

Also called: prairie gentian
Features: beautiful blue, purple, pink, yellow or white flowers **Height:** 8–36"
Spread: usually half the height

Moss Rose

Portulaca

*F*or a brilliant show in the hottest, driest, most neglected area of the garden, you can't go wrong with moss rose.

Growing

Moss rose requires **full sun**. The soil should be of **poor fertility, sandy** and **well drained**. If you sow directly outdoors, rain may transport the tiny seeds to unexpected places. To ensure that you have plants where you want them, start the seed indoors. Moss rose also self-seeds, often providing a colorful show year after year.

Tips

Moss rose grows well under the eaves of a house or in a dry, rocky, exposed area. It also makes a great addition to a hanging basket on a sunny front porch. Remember to water it occasionally. As long as the location is sunny, this plant does well with minimal care.

Recommended

P. grandiflora forms a bushy mound of succulent foliage. It bears delicate, papery, rose-like flowers profusely all summer. Many cultivars are available, including ones with flowers that stay open on cloudy days.

P. grandiflora (above & below)

For an interesting and attractive effect, moss rose plants can be placed close together and allowed to intertwine.

Also called: portulaca **Features:** drought resistant; red, pink, yellow, white, purple, orange or peach summer flowers **Height:** 4–8" **Spread:** 6–12" or wider

Ornamental Kale

Brassica

B. oleracea cultivar (above & below)

Ornamental kale has stunning variegated foliage and is wonderful in containers and flower boxes.

Growing

Ornamental kale prefers **full sun** but tolerates partial shade. The soil should be **neutral to slightly alkaline, fertile** and **moist** yet **well drained**. For best results, fertilize a few times through winter.

Ornamental kale plants can be started in trays and transplanted in fall. Many packages of seeds contain a variety of cultivars.

The plant colors brighten after a light frost or when the air temperature drops below 50° F.

Tips

Ornamental kale is a tough, bold plant that is at home in both vegetable gardens and flowerbeds.

Wait until some true leaves develop before thinning. When thinning seedlings, use the discards in salads.

Recommended

B. oleracea (**Acephala Group**) forms loose, erect rosettes of large, often-fringed leaves in shades of purple, red, pink and white. It grows 12–24" tall, with an equal spread. **Osaka Series** plants grow 12" tall and wide, with wavy leaves that are red to pink in the center and blue to green near the edges.

Features: edible, colorful foliage
Height: 12–24" **Spread:** 12–24"

Pansy • Johnny-Jump-Up
Viola

Pansy and Johnny-jump-up are popular winter garden staples. When they reseed, they create dazzling displays in odd places such as gravel driveways, between evergreen shrubs and in sidewalk cracks.

Growing
*Viola*s prefer **full sun** but tolerate partial shade. The soil should be **fertile, moist** yet **well drained**.

These plants do best in cool weather and die back completely in our hot summers.

Tips
*Viola*s can be used in beds, borders and containers, and they look great mixed in with spring-flowering bulbs. Pinch off the flower buds of new transplants to create larger, bushier plants.

Recommended
V. tricolor (Johnny-jump-up) is a popular species. The flowers are usually a combination of purple, white and yellow, but several varieties have one-color flowers, often purple.

V. x *wittrockiana* (pansy) offers blue, purple, red, orange, yellow, pink and white flowers, often multi-colored or with face-like markings. Many, many cultivars are available.

V. x *wittrockiana* cultivar (above), *V. tricolor* (below)

Sow the seeds indoors in mid-summer for fall and early-winter blooms. They germinate best if kept in darkness until they sprout.

Features: blue, purple, red, orange, yellow, pink, white or multi-colored flowers; easy to grow; cold hardy **Height:** 3–10"
Spread: 6–12"

Petunia
Petunia

Milliflora type 'Fantasy' (above), Multiflora type (below)

For speedy growth, prolific bloom-ing and ease of care, petunias are hard to beat. Even the most neglected plants bloom all summer.

Growing
Petunias prefer **full sun**. The soil should be of **average fertility, light, sandy** and **well drained**. In mid-summer, pinch the plant back halfway or cut the blooms for arrangements, thereby keeping the plant compact and bushy and encouraging new growth and flowers.

When sowing, press the seeds into the soil surface but don't cover them with soil.

Tips
Use petunias in beds, borders, contain-ers and hanging baskets.

Recommended
P. x *hybrida* is a large group of popular annuals. It is important to choose plants that can take our summer weather. **Grandifloras** have the largest flowers but can be damaged by high heat, humidity and rain. **Millifloras,** such as the **Fantasy Series,** have the smallest flowers and are the least likely to suffer in our summers. **Multifloras** bear inter-mediate sizes and numbers of flowers and suffer intermediate rain damage; any of the **Wave Series** are excellent choices. For cascading plants, look for the **Supertunia** or **Surfinia Series** plants. Some varieties, especially those with purple or white flowers, are very fragrant.

Features: pink, purple, red, white, yellow, coral, blue or bicolored flowers; versatility
Height: 6–18" **Spread:** 12–24" or wider

Polka Dot Plant

Hypoestes

As gardeners become increasingly aware that attractive foliage is a key component of good garden design, polka dot plant is enjoying increasing popularity as a foliage plant.

Growing
Polka dot plant prefers **partial shade** but tolerates full sun; dense shade reduces leaf coloration and encourages floppy growth. The soil should be of **average fertility, humus rich, moist** and **well drained**. Seed indoors in early spring.

Pinch the growing tips frequently to encourage bushy growth. Pinch off the inconspicuous flowers, or the plants may decline.

Tips
Polka dot plant can be used in small groups as accent plants, in mass plantings and in mixed containers. In general, it looks best planted in clusters rather than singly. Polka dot plant is often grown as a houseplant and does best in a sunny window.

Recommended
H. phyllostachya (*H. sanguinolenta*) is a bushy plant grown for its attractive foliage. The mostly green leaves are lightly dusted with pink spots. **Confetti Series** foliage is heavily spotted with light or dark pink or white. **Splash Series** plants are compact, with foliage that is brightly streaked and spotted with pink, white or red.

H. phyllostachya Confetti Series (above)
H. phyllostachya 'Pink Splash'

Add zip to your impatiens with polka dot plant.

Features: colorful pink-, red- or white-marked foliage **Height:** 12–24" **Spread:** 12–18"

Primrose

Primula

P. veris (above & below)

The edible young leaves of P. veris *can be added to salads for a hint of spice.*

Primroses enjoy cool locations, which, unfortunately often doom them in our hot, humid summers. Given a cool, moist setting, primroses will reward you with extended blooming.

Growing

Grow primroses in **partial shade**, in **moderately fertile, humus-rich, neutral to slightly acidic, moist, well-drained** soil. Primroses are not drought resistant, and they quickly wilt and fade if not watered regularly.

Tips

Primroses work well in many parts of the garden. Try them in a woodland area or under the shade of taller shrubs and perennials in a border or rock garden.

Temperatures too low or high halt blooming. Plant primroses in a variety of sites to increase your chances of success.

Recommended

P. veris (cowslip primrose) is a perennial that we grow as an annual. It forms a rosette of deeply veined, crinkled foliage. Small clusters of tubular, yellow flowers are borne at the tops of narrow stems.

Features: colorful flowers in yellow, often with shades of red or orange **Height:** 5–10" **Spread:** 5–10"

Rocket Larkspur
Annual Delphinium

Consolida

Rocket larkspur is an excellent choice for the back of the garden, delivering a strong vertical accent. All varieties are great for cutting.

Growing

Rocket larkspur does equally well in **full sun** or **light shade**. The soil should be **fertile, rich in organic matter** and **well drained**. Keep the roots cool and add a light mulch; dried grass clippings or shredded leaves work well. Don't mulch too close to the base of the plant, or crown rot may develop.

Sow the seeds in peat pots to prevent root damage when transplanting. Seeds started indoors do best if chilled in the refrigerator for one week prior to sowing.

Deadhead to prolong the blooming period.

Tips

Plant groups of larkspurs in mixed borders or cottage gardens. The tallest varieties may require staking.

Recommended

C. ambigua (*C. ajacis*) is an upright plant with spikes of flowers held above feathery foliage. Cultivars range in height from dwarfs 12" tall to giants 4' tall.

Larkspurs are sentimental favorites of many gardeners who remember them from grandmother's garden.

C. ambigua cultivar (above & below)

Features: blue, purple, pink, gray, white or bicolored flowers; attractive habit
Height: 12"–4' **Spread:** 6–14"

Snapdragon
Antirrhinum

A. *majus* cultivar (above & below)

Snapdragon is a popular and appealing plant. The flower colors are always rich and vibrant, and even the most jaded gardeners are tempted to squeeze open the dragons' mouths.

Growing
Snapdragon prefers **full sun** but tolerates light or partial shade. The soil should be of **average fertility, neutral to** alkaline and **well drained;** this plant does not perform well in acidic soil. Do not cover the seeds when sowing, because they require light to germinate.

To encourage bushy growth, pinch the tips of the young plants. Cut off the flower spikes as they fade to promote further blooming and to prevent the plant from dying back before the end of the season.

Snapdragons grow and look their best when they're planted annually.

Tips
Short varieties work well near the front of a border, and the tallest ones look good in the back. The dwarf and medium-height varieties can be used in planters. Trailing varieties do well in hanging baskets.

Recommended
Many cultivars of **A. *majus*** are available. They are generally grouped into dwarf, medium and giant size categories.

Features: entertaining white, cream, yellow, orange, red, maroon, pink, purple or bicolored summer flowers **Height:** 6"–4' **Spread:** 6–24"

Spider Flower

Cleome

C. hassleriana Royal Queen Series (above), *C. hassleriana* (below)

Southern gardeners long ago caught on to the special allure and charm of spider flower.

Growing

Spider flower prefers **full sun** but tolerates partial shade. It adapts to most **well-drained** soils. Although drought tolerant, this plant performs best with regular water; mix in organic matter to help retain soil moisture. Pinch out the tip of the center stem on young plants to encourage branching and more blooms. Deadhead to prolong blooming and reduce prolific self-seeding.

Tips

Spider flower can be planted in groups at the back of a border or in the center of an island bed. It makes an attractive addition to a large mixed container.

Recommended

C. hassleriana is a tall, upright plant with strong, supple, thorny stems. The foliage and flowers of this plant have a strong but not unpleasant scent. **'Helen Campbell'** has white flowers. **Royal Queen Series** has flowers in purple, pink or white. Plants in this series resist fading. **'Sparkler Blush'** is a dwarf cultivar with pink flowers that fade to white.

Spider flower provides hummingbirds with nectar often into early fall.

Features: attractive, scented foliage; purple, pink or white flowers; thorny stems
Height: 3–5' **Spread:** 18–36"

Sweet William

Dianthus

D. barbatus cultivar (above & below)

Sweet William blooms in spring, so it is a candidate for fall planting alongside pansies and snapdragons. Look for it in garden centers as early as possible. Most selections are tall plants, but much breeding has been done to draw down the height and lengthen the flowering time.

Growing

Sweet William prefers **full sun** but tolerates some light shade. A **light, humus-rich, neutral to alkaline, well-drained** soil is preferred. Growing this plant in slightly alkaline soil produces excellent color over a long period. Keep it **sheltered** from strong winds.

To prolong blooming, deadhead as the flowers fade. With a few flowers left in place to mature, this plant self-seeds quite easily. The seedlings may differ from the parent plants, often with new and interesting results.

Tips

Sweet William is great for mass planting, in rock gardens, for edging flower borders and walkways and as a cut flower.

Recommended

D. barbatus bears flattened clusters of often two-toned flowers in white, pink, red or purple-red.

The tiny, delicate petals of sweet William can be used to decorate cakes, but be sure to remove the bitter white part at the petal base.

Features: white, pink, red or purple flowers; easy to grow   **Height:** 18–24"
Spread: 10–12"

Verbena

Verbena

*T*his annual demands dry, well-drained soil, so it is best grown on sunny mounds, along raised median strips, under eaves or with plants that suck moisture out of the soil, such as junipers.

Growing

Verbenas grow best in **full sun**. The soil should be **fertile** and **very well drained**. Pinch back young plants for bushy growth.

Tips

Use verbenas on rock walls and in beds, borders, rock gardens, containers, hanging baskets and window boxes. They make good substitutes for ivy-leaved geranium in places where the sun is hot and where a roof overhang keeps the mildew-prone verbenas dry.

Recommended

V. x *hybrida* is a bushy plant that may be upright or spreading. It bears clusters of small flowers in a wide range of colors. Many cultivars are available. **Sandy Series** plants produce flowers in white, magenta and scarlet.

V. x *hybrida* cultivar (above & below)

To encourage a lot of fall blooms and good air circulation, cut verbenas back by one-half in mid-summer.

Also called: garden verbena **Features:** red, pink, purple, blue, yellow, scarlet, peach or white summer flowers, some with white centers and some tinged with silver
Height: 8"–15" **Spread:** 12"

Wallflower

Erysimum

E. x allionii (above & below)

The vivid colors of wallflower make it a great addition to any garden. Let it self-sow, or collect the seeds and sow them yourself.

Growing

Grow wallflower plants in **full sun,** in **moderately fertile, neutral to alkaline, moist, well-drained** soil. Ensure you provide adequate water.

The plants can be lightly trimmed after flowering to promote more blooms and to keep the plant tidy.

Tips

Wallflower is great for beds or borders. It is also effective in rock gardens, on rock walls and in containers, and it is a good cut flower.

Recommended

E.* x *allionii (*E. hieraciifolium, Cherianthus allonii*) is an upright, evergreen perennial that we grow as an annual. It self-sows in much of Georgia. Clusters of fragrant, orange to yellow flowers bloom in spring.

The name 'wallflower' arises from the penchant of the plant to grow in old walls, on rock faces and in quarries—not from any comparison to shy people at dances.

Features: bright yellow, orange, red, cream, bronze, burgundy or brown flowers
Height: 12–24" **Spread:** 8–18"

Wishbone Flower

Torenia

*W*ishbone flower comes in several deeply colored cultivars. Be sure to point them out to children, who are often intrigued by familiar shapes showing up in strange places.

Growing

Wishbone flower prefers **light shade** but tolerates partial to full shade; in partial shade, ensure **protection** from the hot afternoon sun is provided. The soil should be **fertile, light, humus rich** and **moist**. This plant requires regular watering.

Don't cover the seeds when planting; they require light to germinate.

Tips

Wishbone flower is very soothing and subtle, and it blends well in a shade garden. It can be massed in a shaded bed or border, used as an edging plant or added to mixed containers and hanging baskets.

Recommended

T. fournieri is a bushy, rounded to upright plant. Its purple flowers have yellow throats. **Clown Series** plants are compact and feature flowers in purple, blue, pink or white. '**Summer Wave Blue**' is an outstanding plant for Georgia gardens. It bears large, deep blue flowers.

T. fournieri cultivar (above & below)

Wishbone flower gets its name from the arrangement of the stamens (male parts) in the center of the flower.

Features: attractive, interesting purple, pink, blue, burgundy, white or bicolored flowers with a yellow spot on the lower petal **Height:** 6–12"
Spread: 6–8"

Zinnia
Zinnia

Z. elegans 'Profusion White' (above)
Z. elegans mixed cultivars (below)

*Z*innias have a wide range of uses in both formal and informal gardens, in containers and as cut flowers.

Growing
Zinnias grow best in **full sun,** in **fertile, moist, well-drained** soil rich in **organic matter.** Deadhead to prolong blooming and to keep the plants looking neat.

Zinnias grow very well when direct sown in the garden. To avoid disturbing the roots when transplanting seedlings started early, sow the seeds in individual peat pots.

Tips
Zinnias are useful in beds, borders, containers and cutting gardens. The dwarf selections can be used as edging plants. Choose mildew-resistant plants, grow them in locations with good air circulation and avoid wetting the foliage.

Recommended
Z. angustifolia (narrow-leaf zinnia) is an erect, self-grooming, disease-free plant that bears bright orange flowers with centers of deep purple and orange.

Z. elegans is a bushy, upright plant with daisy-like flowers in a variety of forms. **Profusion Series** hybrids are fast-growing, mildew-resistant, compact plants with bright cherry red, orange or white flowers.

Z. haageana (Mexican zinnia) is a bushy plant with narrow leaves. The bright, daisy-like, bicolored or tricolored flowers come in shades of orange, red, yellow, maroon, brown or gold.

Features: bushy plants; colorful flowers, often bicolored or tricolored, in shades of red, yellow, green, purple, orange, pink, white, maroon, brown or gold **Height:** 6"–4' **Spread:** 12"

Aster

Aster

Purple and pink asters make a nice contrast to the yellow-flowered perennials common in the late-summer garden, and they also attract a plethora of birds, butterflies and bees.

Growing

Asters prefer **full sun** but tolerate partial shade. The soil should be **fertile**, **moist** and **well drained**. Divide every two to three years to control spread and maintain vigor, or the plants will decline rapidly. The tall selections require staking.

Tips

Plant asters in the middle and back of borders and in cottage gardens, or naturalize them in wild gardens.

Recommended

A. novae-angliae (Michaelmas daisy, New England aster) is an upright, spreading, clump-forming perennial that bears yellow-centered, purple flowers. Cultivars come in many sizes and produce masses of flowers in white as well as in many shades of purple and pink.

A. novae-angliae (above), A. *novi-belgii* (below)

For bushy, compact aster plants that don't need staking and have more blooms and reduced disease problems, use hedge shears to cut them back in early spring and late spring.

Features: late-summer to mid-fall flowers in white, purple or pink, often with yellow centers **Height:** 10"–6' **Spread:** 2–4' **Hardiness:** zones 4–8

Black-Eyed Susan
Rudbeckia

R. fulgida var. *sullivantii* 'Goldsturm' with purple coneflower (above), *R. nitida* 'Herbstsonne' (below)

Black-eyed Susans are tough, low-maintenance, long-lived perennials. Plant them wherever you want a casual look. Black-eyed Susans look great planted in drifts, which can develop from the modest beginnings of as few as three plants.

Growing

Black-eyed Susans grow well in **full sun** in **well-drained** soil of **average fertility**. Several *Rudbeckia* species are touted as 'claybusters' for their tolerance of fairly heavy clay soils. Established plants are somewhat drought tolerant but prefer to have regular water. Divide in spring or fall, every three to five years, and don't hesitate to consign a few pieces to the compost heap.

Tips

Include these native plants in wildflower and natural gardens, beds and borders. Pinching the plants in June results in shorter, bushier stands. The flowers last well when cut for arrangements.

Recommended

R. fulgida var. *sullivantii* **'Goldsturm'** is an upright, spreading plant 24–36" tall that bears large, bright, golden yellow to orange-yellow flowers with brown centers. (Zones 3–8)

R. laciniata (cutleaf coneflower) forms a large, open clump up to 8' tall. The yellow flowers have green centers. **'Goldquelle'** grows 2–4' tall and has bright yellow, double flowers. (Zones 3–8)

R. nitida is an upright, spreading plant 5–7' tall, with green-centered, yellow flowers. **'Herbstsonne'** ('Autumn Sun') has bright, golden yellow flowers. (Zones 4–9)

Features: bright yellow or orange flowers with brown or green centers; attractive foliage; easy to grow **Height:** 2–8' **Spread:** 18–36" **Hardiness:** zones 3–8

Blackberry Lily

Belamcanda chinensis

B. chinensis 'Mixed Colors' (above), *B. chinensis* (below)

Blackberry lily is a good, all-round perennial that has attractive foliage, colorful flowers and interesting fruit. Don't worry that this wonderful plant is short-lived, because it self-seeds enough to keep both you and your friends in plants.

Growing

Blackberry lily grows well in **full sun** or **partial shade,** in **moist, well-drained** soil of **average fertility,** with a lot of **organic matter** mixed in. It can adapt to sandy soils and some clay soils if enough organic matter is added. Plants may need staking when grown in rich soil.

Blackberry lily can be propagated by dividing the rhizomes in spring, or it can easily be grown from seed.

Tips

Blackberry lily is used to provide a vertical element in mixed beds and borders.

Recommended

B. chinensis forms clumps of sword-shaped, green foliage that is arranged in fans like those of iris plants. Above the foliage rise clusters of star-shaped, yellow to orange flowers with red or maroon spots. In fall, the fruit splits open to reveal shiny black berries.

Actually not a lily, blackberry lily is a member of the iris family.

Features: bright yellow or orange summer flowers; fall fruit; attractive foliage; easy to grow **Height:** 24–36" **Spread:** 12–18" **Hardiness:** zones: 5–9

Blanket Flower

Gaillardia

G. x *grandiflora* (above)
G. x *grandiflora* 'Baby Cole' (below)

Blanket flower's multi-colored flowerheads add a fiery glow to cottage gardens and meadow plantings. When seen growing in sunny, tough spots, it's easy to imagine the flowers are fake.

Blanket flower is a workhorse in any garden. It thrives on neglect and produces an abundance of flowers over a long period, even if not dead-headed.

Growing

Blanket flower prefers **full sun,** in **well-drained, poor to moderately fertile** soil. Blanket flower may be short-lived, but it happily reseeds itself. It tolerates drought and heat.

Don't cover the seeds, which need light to germinate. Propagate by division or root cuttings in spring.

Tips

Blanket flower has an informal, sprawling habit that makes it a perfect addition to an informal cottage garden or mixed border. It can be used on exposed, sunny slopes to help reduce erosion while more permanent plants grow in.

To reduce pest or disease problems, avoid overwatering. Plant blanket flower where it will not get watered with other plants. Once established, the less water this plant receives, the better it does.

Recommended

G. x *grandiflora* is a bushy, clump-forming perennial that grows 24–36" tall and 18–24" wide. The flowers are red, orange and yellow, with yellow-brown to reddish centers.

Features: bright flowers in red, orange or yellow, often in combination; easy to grow
Height: 8–36" **Spread:** 18–24"
Hardiness: zones: 3–9

Blazing Star
Liatris

The fuzzy, spiked blossoms of blazing star make outstanding cut flowers. Blazing star is also excellent for attracting butterflies.

Growing

Blazing star prefers **full sun**. The soil should be of **average fertility, humus rich, sandy** and **well drained**. Water well during the growing season but don't allow this plant to stand in water during winter's cool weather. Mulch during summer to prevent moisture loss.

Trim off the spent flower spikes to promote a longer blooming period and to keep blazing star looking tidy. Divide in fall, every three or four years, when the clump begins to appear crowded.

Tips

Use blazing star in borders and meadow plantings. To avoid root rot in winter, choose a location with good drainage. Blazing star grows well in planters. Mix the spikes of blazing star with daisy-shaped flowers for added drama.

Recommended

L. spicata is an erect, clump-forming plant. The flowers are pinkish purple or white. **'Floristan White'** has white flowers. **'Kobold'** is a slightly smaller plant with deep purple flowers.

L. spicata 'Kobold' (above), *L. spicata* (below)

Blazing star's flower spikes make excellent, long-lasting cut flowers.

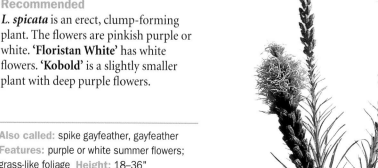

Also called: spike gayfeather, gayfeather
Features: purple or white summer flowers; grass-like foliage **Height:** 18–36"
Spread: 18–24" **Hardiness:** zones 3–9

Blue Star
Amsonia

A. tabernaemontana

Perennials are not known for spectacular fall color, but blue star breaks the mold. With its spectacular display of stunning, golden yellow hues, nothing in the fall partial shade garden is showier than the foliage of blue star.

Growing

Blue star grows well in **full sun, partial shade** or **light shade;** too much shade can produce floppy plants. The soil should be of **average fertility, slightly acidic, moist** and **well drained,** although *A. tabernaemontana* tolerates drought once established. Propagate more plants from seed or by division in spring.

Blue star is native to the southeastern United States.

Tips

These pretty plants have a fine, billowy appearance. Plant them in groups of three to five to achieve the most stunning results.

Recommended

A. hubrichtii (Arkansas bluestar) grows 3–4' tall and 4' wide, bearing star-shaped, light blue to white blooms. These plants prefer a moist soil. The narrow, feathery leaves turn yellow gold in fall. (Zones 5–9)

A. tabernaemontana (willow bluestar) prefers sun but does well in partial shade. It grows 24–36" tall and up to 5' wide, producing small, lavender blue flowers. **Var.** *salicifolia* has narrower foliage and more open clusters of flowers than the species.

Features: blue spring and summer flowers; attractive habit and foliage **Height:** 2–4' **Spread:** 2–5' **Hardiness:** zones 3–9

Boltonia

Boltonia

Boltonia is a tall, easy-to-grow, pest- and disease-free plant that blooms profusely, bringing fresh color to the late-season garden for four weeks or more.

Growing

Boltonia prefers **full sun** and **fertile, humus rich, moist, well-drained** soil. It tolerates partial shade, adapts to less fertile soils and even tolerates some drought. When the clump is overgrown or dying out in the middle, divide in fall or early spring.

The stout stems rarely require staking. If the plants grow too tall for your liking, cut the stems back by one-third in June.

Tips

This large plant suits the middle or back of a mixed border, a naturalized or cottage garden or a site near a pond or other water feature. A good alternative to the taller asters, boltonia is less susceptible to powdery mildew.

Recommended

B. asteroides is a large, upright perennial up to 6' tall, with narrow, grayish green leaves. It bears daisy-like, white or slightly purple flowers with yellow centers. **'Snowbank'** is the best boltonia for Southern gardens. It has a denser, more compact habit, growing only 3–4' tall, and bears more plentiful flowers than the species.

B. asteroides (above & below)

In the heat of late summer, boltonia's perky blossoms make even the hottest days seem cooler.

Features: late-summer and fall flowers in white, mauve or pink, with yellow centers; easy to grow **Height:** 3–6' **Spread:** up to 4' **Hardiness:** zones: 4–9

Butterfly Weed

Asclepias

A. tuberosa (above & below)

Butterfly weed, a North American native, will attract butterflies to your garden. It is a major food source for the monarch butterfly.

Growing

Butterfly weed prefers **full sun** and **well-drained** soil. It tolerates drought once established but enjoys some moisture in an extended drought. The deep taproot makes division very difficult. To propagate, use the seedlings that sprout up around the base of the plant.

Deadhead to encourage a second blooming.

Tips

Use butterfly weed in meadow plantings and borders, on dry banks, in neglected areas and in wildflower, cottage and butterfly gardens.

Butterfly weed is slow to start in spring. To avoid inadvertently digging it up, place a marker beside each plant in fall.

Recommended

A. tuberosa forms a clump of upright, leafy stems. It bears clusters of orange flowers from mid-summer to early fall. A variety of cultivars offer solid or bicolored flowers in shades of scarlet, gold, orange or pink.

Be careful not to pick off or destroy the green-and-black-striped caterpillars that feed on butterfly weed—they will become beautiful monarch butterflies.

Also called: milkweed, pleurisy root
Features: orange, yellow, red, pink or bicolored flowers; attractive form **Height:** 18–36"
Spread: 12–24" **Hardiness:** zones 3–9

Cheddar Pink

Dianthus

D. gratianopolitanus 'Bath's Pink' (above & below)

The tough-as-nails 'Bath's Pink' is an outstanding perennial selection for Georgia. It requires minimal care, has outstanding foliage and explodes with color and fragrance every spring!

Growing

Cheddar pink prefers **full sun** in a **neutral to alkaline, well-drained** soil. Ensure excellent drainage—these plants hate to stand in water.

Tips

Use cheddar pink in rock gardens, on rock walls, for edging borders and walkways, in cutting gardens and even as a groundcover. To prolong blooming, deadhead as the flowers fade.

Recommended

D. gratianopolitanus (cheddar pink) is long-lived and forms a very dense, spreading mat of 4–8" tall, evergreen, silver gray foliage with sweet-scented flowers, usually in shades of pink. **'Bath's Pink'** can reach 10" tall, has blue-green foliage and bears an abundance of light to medium pink flowers. **'Firewitch'** ('Feuerhexe') is an upright selection that bears rosy pink flowers.

Features: pink, red, white or purple early-spring flowers; attractive foliage
Height: 4–10" **Spread:** 6–18"
Hardiness: zones 3–9

Columbine

Aquilegia

A. canadensis (left & right)

Delicate but long-lasting columbine flowers herald the passing of spring and the arrival of warm summer weather.

Growing

Columbines grow well in **light or partial shade,** in **fertile, moist, well-drained** soil, but they adapt to most soil conditions. They can be grown in full sun if the soil remains moist. Division is not required but can be done to propagate desirable plants. Divided plants may take a while to recover, because columbines dislike having their roots disturbed.

Columbines self-seed but are not invasive. Any seedlings that turn up can be transplanted.

Tips

Use columbines in rock gardens, formal or casual borders, naturalized areas or woodland gardens.

Columbines may be bothered by leaf miners. Cut off and remove damaged foliage.

Recommended

A. canadensis (wild columbine, Canada columbine) is a native plant common in woodlands and fields. It grows 24–36" tall and bears yellow flowers with red-orange spurs. **'Corbett'** grows 18–24" tall and bears light yellow flowers.

Features: red and yellow flowers in spring and summer; attractive foliage **Height:** 18–36" **Spread:** 12–16" **Hardiness:** zones 3–9

Coreopsis
Coreopsis

The bright and cheerful flowers of coreopsis make a fabulous addition to every garden.

Growing

These plants grow best in **full sun** or **partial shade**. The soil should be of **average fertility, sandy, light** and **well drained**. Moist, cool locations with heavy soil can promote crown rot. Too fertile a soil or too shaded a location encourages floppy growth. Deadhead to keep the plants blooming.

Tips

Coreopsis are versatile plants, useful in formal and informal borders, in rock gardens, in meadow plantings and in cottage gardens.

Recommended

C. auriculata 'Nana' (mouse-eared tickseed) grows about 12" tall and spreads indefinitely, although slowly. It bears yellow-orange flowers in late spring.

C. verticillata (thread-leaf coreopsis) is a mound-forming plant with attractive, finely divided foliage and bright yellow summer flowers. It grows 24–32" tall and 18" wide. **'Golden Showers'** bears large, deep yellow flowers. **'Moonbeam'** bears creamy yellow flowers and does best with protection from the hot afternoon sun. **'Zagreb'** has golden yellow flowers on plants 12" tall and wide.

C. auriculata 'Nana' (above)
C. grandiflora (below)

Mass plant coreopsis to fill in a dry, exposed bank where nothing else will grow—and enjoy the bright, sunny flowers all summer long.

Also called: tickseed **Features:** late-spring or summer flowers in yellow or orange; attractive foliage **Height:** 12–32"
Spread: 12–24" **Hardiness:** zones 4–9

Daylily

Hemerocallis

'Dewey Roquemore' (above), 'Bonanza' (below)

Easygoing, adaptive and versatile, daylilies are so tough they can even be dug up and moved while in full bloom.

Adaptable, durable and very popular, daylilies are easy to fit into any garden.

Growing

Daylilies bear the most flowers in **full sun** but also grow in partial shade. The soil should be **fertile, moist** and **well drained,** but these plants adapt to most conditions and are hard to kill once established. Although daylilies can be left indefinitely without dividing, you can divide them every two to three years to keep them vigorous or to propagate them.

Tips

Plant daylilies in borders and beds or use them on banks and in ditches to control erosion. They can be naturalized in woodland or meadow gardens. Small varieties look nice in planters.

Deadhead to prolong blooming. Be careful when deadheading purple-flowered daylilies, because the sap can stain fingers and clothes. Once blooming is complete and the foliage begins turning yellow, daylilies can be pruned right to the ground for a second flush of beautiful growth until frost.

Recommended

Coming in a range of species, cultivars and hybrids, daylilies offer an almost infinite number of forms, sizes and colors. See your local garden center or daylily grower to find out what's available.

Features: spring and summer flowers in every color except blue; grass-like foliage; easy to grow **Height:** 1–4' **Spread:** 1–4' **Hardiness:** zones 3–9

Evening Primrose

Oenothera

Evening primrose and sun-drops are native plants that do very well in our Georgia gardens.

Growing

These plants prefer **full sun**. The soil should be of **poor to average fertility** and **very well drained**. In fertile soil, these plants can become invasive. They aren't bothered by hot, humid weather. Divide in spring.

Tips

Use these plants in the front of a border and to edge borders and pathways. Sundrops will brighten a gravelly bank or rock garden.

Evening primrose can be a bit invasive, self-seeding readily and finding its way into unexpected places. Don't be afraid of this spreading plant; just pull out what isn't needed and give it away or compost it.

O. speciosa 'Siskiyou Pink' (above)
O. fruticosa (below)

Recommended

O. fruticosa (sundrops) grows 12–18" tall and wide. It bears bright yellow flowers in summer. The foliage of this plant turns red after a light frost. 'Fireworks' has red stems and yellow blooms that open from red buds.

O. speciosa (showy evening primrose) is a lanky, upright or spreading plant. It grows 10–12" tall and wide. Its flowers can be pink or white.

The flowers of some species of Oenothera *emit phosphorescent light, giving rise to another common name: evening star.*

Also called: sundrops **Features:** yellow, pink or white summer flowers; easy to grow **Height:** 10–18" **Spread:** 10–18" **Hardiness:** zones 3–8

False Indigo

Baptisia

B. *australis* (above & below)

False indigo is another beautiful Georgia native that requires minimal care and provides years of enjoyment. Be patient, though, because young plants may take a few years to grow large enough to flower.

Growing

False indigo prefers **full sun** but tolerates partial shade; too much shade causes lank growth that flops over easily. The soil should be of **poor to average fertility, sandy** and **well drained**.

Tips

False indigo can be used in an informal border or a cottage garden. It is an attractive addition to a naturalized planting, on a slope or in any sunny, well-drained spot.

Recommended

B. australis is an upright or somewhat spreading, clump-forming plant that bears spikes of purple-blue flowers in early summer. The swollen seedpods provide interest in late summer and fall. **'Purple Smoke'** is a hybrid with *B. australis* as one of the parents. It has smoky purple-white flowers.

If you've had difficulties growing lupines, try the far less demanding false indigo instead.

Features: late-spring or early-summer flowers in purple-blue or purple-white; attractive habit and foliage; seedpods **Height:** 3–5' **Spread:** 2–4' **Hardiness:** zones 3–8

Goldenrod
Solidago & Solidaster

The cultivated varieties of goldenrods tame the unruly appearance of the species but keep the profusion of bloom.

Growing

Goldenrods prefer **full sun** and tolerate partial shade. The soil should be of **poor to average fertility, light** and **well drained**. Too fertile a soil results in lush growth, few flowers and invasive behavior.

To keep the plants vigorous, and to control growth, divide them every three to five years in spring or fall.

Tips

Goldenrods are great for providing late-season color. They look at home in a large border or in a cottage or wild-flower garden. Don't plant them near less vigorous plants, because goldenrod can quickly overwhelm them. Goldenrod is a great plant for xeriscaping.

Recommended

Solidago **hybrids** form a clump of strong stems with narrow leaves. They grow about 2–4' tall and about 18–24" wide. Plume-like clusters of yellow flowers are produced from mid-summer to fall. **'Crown of Rays'** holds its flower clusters in horizontal spikes. **'Golden Shower'** bears flowers in horizontal or drooping plumes.

x *Solidaster luteus* is a hybrid genus of a *Solidago* species and an *Aster* species. Growing 24–30" tall and wide, it bears daisy-like, pale yellow flowers with darker yellow centers.

S. 'Crown of Rays' (above & below)

Ragweed (Ambrosia species), not goldenrod, is the source of hay-fever pollen.

Features: yellow mid-summer to fall flowers; attractive habit **Height:** 24"–4'
Spread: 18–30" **Hardiness:** zones 3–8

Hardy Ageratum
Eupatorium coelestinum

E. coelestinum species and white-flowered cultivar (above), *E. coelestinum* (below)

Hardy ageratum is the most heat tolerant of the *Eupatorium* species. Sometimes considered weedy, this easy-to-grow plant is a great choice for cool fall color.

Growing
Hardy ageratum grows well in **full sun** or **partial shade,** in **fertile, moist** soil. Wet or dry soils are tolerated.

Hardy ageratum tends to be a bit lanky in growth, but it can be cut or sheared back several times to create bushier plants and more flowers. To allow flowering, stop cutting back by mid- to late July.

Tips
Hardy ageratum can be used in a bed or border, at the edge of a woodland garden or near a pond or other water feature.

Hardy ageratum can be prevented from spreading by planting it in a contained area where the rhizomes are restricted from spreading.

Recommended
E. coelestinum (hardy ageratum) is a bushy, upright plant that spreads by shallow rhizomes. It bears clusters of flossy, light blue to lavender flowers.

Also called: mistflower, blue mistflower
Features: light blue to lavender flowers in late summer and fall; attractive foliage and habit; easy to grow **Height:** 24–36"
Spread: 24–36" **Hardiness:** zones 6–10

Hosta

Hosta

Breeders are always looking for new variations in hosta foliage. Swirls, stripes, puckers and ribs enhance the various leaf sizes, shapes and colors.

Growing

Hostas prefer **light or partial shade** but will grow in full shade. Morning sun is preferable to afternoon sun. The soil should ideally be **fertile, moist** and **well drained,** but most soils are tolerated. Hostas are fairly drought tolerant, especially if mulched to help retain moisture.

Division is not required but can be done every few years in early spring to propagate new plants.

Tips

Hostas make wonderful woodland plants. They look very attractive when combined with ferns and other fine-textured plants, and the evergreen, tropical-like foliage of lenten rose. Hostas work well in mixed borders, particularly when used to hide the leggy lower stems and branches that some shrubs develop. The dense growth and thick, shade-providing leaves of hostas help suppress weeds, but slugs, deer and voles consider hostas to be a tasty snack.

Recommended

Hundreds of hosta species, cultivars and hybrids exist. Visit your local garden center, go online or get a mail-order catalog to find out what's available.

H. fortunei 'Francee' (above)

If you think hosta's flowers clash with the foliage, removing the newly emerged flower stems won't harm the plant and is actually helpful during a drought.

Also called: plantain lily, funkia
Features: decorative foliage; white or purple summer and fall flowers **Height:** 4–36"
Spread: 6"–6' **Hardiness:** zones 3–9

Japanese Anemone
Anemone

A. x *hybrida* (above & below)

Often considered some of the most beautiful flowers, anemones are also some of the last plants to stop flowering in late fall. Anemones may need more than one year to take off, but it's worth the wait.

Growing

Anemones grow well in **partial or light shade,** in **humus-rich, moist, well-drained** soil. Provide **protection** from the hot mid-day sun. Divide in early spring or late fall; grow the divisions in containers for a year before replanting them in spring.

Tips

Anemones make beautiful additions to lightly shaded borders, woodland gardens and rock gardens. They look magnificent when planted en masse. To support the tall stems of Japanese anemone, you can plant it behind shrubby roses.

Recommended

A. hupehensis var. *japonica* 'Bressingham Glow' is an erect, clump-forming plant 18–24" wide. It bears deep rose red to raspberry pink, semi-double flowers on 24–30" tall stems.

A. x *hybrida* (Japanese anemone) is an upright, suckering hybrid that grows 3–5' tall, 24–36" wide, and bears pink or white flowers. Many cultivars are available. '**Honorine Jobert**' is a heat-tolerant selection with pure white flowers.

Also called: windflower **Features:** pink, red, purple, blue, yellow or white flowers; attractive foliage **Height:** 2–5' **Spread:** 18–36" **Hardiness:** zones 5–8

Japanese Roof Iris

Iris

*J*apanese roof iris is an easy-to-grow plant that is ideally suited to our Georgia climate.

Growing

Japanese roof iris prefers **full sun** or **partial shade,** in **light, moist, well-drained** soil of **average fertility**. It benefits from a layer of organic mulch that is topped up in spring and fall, but make sure you keep the mulch away from the crown of the plant. The mulch helps prevent possible frost-heaving of the shallow rhizomes.

Divide Japanese roof iris after flowering is complete. Deadhead to keep the plant tidy. Winter-damaged foliage can be cut to within 2" of the ground in spring.

I. tectorum (above & below)

Tips

All irises are popular border plants. Japanese roof iris grows well alongside streams or ponds, and it looks great at the front of a bed or border.

Irises can cause severe internal irritation if ingested. Always wash your hands after handling them. Avoid planting irises where children play.

Recommended

*I. **tectorum*** is a small iris that spreads somewhat quickly by rhizomes. Its sword-shaped, light green foliage is wider than on most other irises. It bears large, flattened, light to dark purple flowers. **'Alba'** ('Album') bears white flowers.

Irises are worth planting for their exotic foliage alone; the blossoms are a bonus.

Features: early-summer flowers in various shades of purple and white; attractive foliage
Height: 10–16" **Spread:** 10–16"
Hardiness: zones 3–8

Joe-Pye Weed
Eupatorium

E. maculatum (above & below)

Joe-Pye weed will attract a plethora of butterflies to your garden.

Joe-Pye weeds are big, bold plants that add volume and stature to the garden and put on a good show of late-season flowers.

Growing

Joe-Pye weeds prefer **full sun** or **partial shade**. The ideal soil is **fertile, neutral to slightly alkaline** and **moist,** but wet soil is tolerated.

Tips

These plants can be used in a moist border or near a pond or other water feature. They work well at the back of a border or in the center of a bed where they can create a backdrop for lower-growing plants.

Recommended

E. maculatum (spotted Joe-Pye weed) grows 5–7' tall and 36" wide, and bears clusters of purple flowers at the ends of purple-spotted stems. **'Gateway'** has reddish stems, grows 4–5' tall and bears much larger, rose pink flower clusters.

E. purpureum (sweet Joe-Pye weed) is a large, robust native plant that grows 6–9' tall and up to 4' wide. It produces clusters of purple flowers at the ends of stems marked with wine purple.

Also called: boneset **Features:** late-summer to fall flowers in white, purple or pink; attractive foliage and habit **Height:** 5–9' **Spread:** 3–4' **Hardiness:** zones 3–9

Lenten Rose

Helleborus

H. orientalis cultivar (left & right)

Beautiful Lenten rose is an early-blooming, relatively problem-free groundcover plant.

Growing

Lenten rose prefers **light, dappled shade to full shade** and a **sheltered** location, but it tolerates some direct sun if the soil stays evenly moist. The soil should be **fertile, humus rich** and **well drained**. Water during establishment and during periods of drought.

Lenten rose dislikes root disturbance and should not be divided. It self-seeds where it is happy, and the small seedlings can be transplanted to other locations.

Tips

Use this plant in a sheltered border or rock garden—or naturalize it in a woodland garden.

Also called: hellebore **Features:** late-winter to spring flowers in white, green, pink, purple or yellow; easy to grow; low maintenance
Height: 15–24" **Spread:** 15–24"
Hardiness: zones 4–9

Any foliage that looks tattered in spring can be trimmed out, allowing new foliage to take its place. If the foliage gets too thick and dense, cut some off to help display the blossoms.

Recommended

H. orientalis is a clump-forming, ever-green perennial. Many cultivars and hybrids are available. The single to double flowers come in a wide range of colors, including white and shades of green, pink, purple and yellow, often in combinations and with spots, streaks or blotches.

*All parts of Lenten rose are **toxic** and can cause dermatitis. Also, the leaf edges can be sharp, so wear long sleeves and gloves when handling these plants.*

Purple Coneflower
Echinacea

E. purpurea 'Magnus' and 'White Swan' (above), *E. purpurea* (below)

Attractive and easy to grow, purple coneflower is a long-lived prairie native that does well in Southern gardens.

Growing

Purple coneflower grows well in **full sun** or **very light shade;** plants in shade may need staking. The soil should be of **average fertility, neutral to slightly alkaline** and **well drained**. The thick taproots help this plant resist drought, but it prefers to have regular water. Divide every four years in spring or fall.

Deadhead to prolong flowering. Leave late-season flowerheads in place to self-seed and attract birds.

Tips

Use purple coneflowers in meadow gardens, beds and borders. They look good massed or as single specimens.

The dry seedheads make an interesting feature in fall and winter gardens.

Recommended

E. purpurea is an upright plant with dark green foliage that bears purple flowers with orangy centers. Some cultivars offer white blooms. White-flowered plants tend to be shorter and not as long-lived as the purple-flowered plants.

Purple coneflower attracts wildlife to the garden; it provides pollen, nectar and seeds for various hungry visitors.

Features: mid-summer to fall flowers in purple, pink or white, with rusty orange centers; persistent seedheads **Height:** 2–5' **Spread:** 12–24" **Hardiness:** zones 3–8

Spiderwort

Tradescantia

Spiderworts are grass-like plants with interesting three-petaled flowers. Spiderworts bloom in the in-between season, when spring flowers are fading and summer blooms haven't yet opened.

Growing

Spiderworts grow equally well in **full sun** or **partial shade,** but they may appreciate some shade from the hot afternoon sun. The soil should be of **average fertility, humus rich** and **moist** but not soaked. If grown in overly rich soil with plentiful water, spiderworts can become weedy and fall open in the center.

To produce a fresh flush of foliage and possibly a second round of blooms late in the season, cut the plants back after flowering has ceased and the leaves fade. Divide in spring or fall every four or so years.

T. x *andersoniana* cultivar (above)
T. x *andersoniana* (below)

Tips

Spiderworts are attractive in a lightly shaded woodland or natural garden, but they also look good in beds and borders. Once established, spiderworts grow almost anywhere. White-flowered spiderworts along a shady woodland path light up a garden.

A related species, T. zebrina, *is often grown as a trailing houseplant.*

Recommended

T.* x *andersoniana forms a large clump of grassy foliage. Clusters of flowers are produced on long stems. Many cultivars are available. One of the parent plants of these hybrids, *T. virginiana,* is native to most of the eastern United States.

Features: purple, blue, pink, red or white early-summer flowers; attractive foliage; easy to grow **Height:** 16–24" **Spread:** 20–30" **Hardiness:** zones 3–9

Stonecrop
Sedum

S. 'Autumn Joy' (above & below)

Tips
Low-growing stonecrops make wonderful ground-covers and additions to rock gardens, rock walls, beds and borders. Taller stonecrops are excellent for a late-season display in a bed or border.

Recommended
Here are several low growing, wide-spreading selections (2–6" tall and 24" wide). **S. acre** (gold moss stonecrop) bears small, yellow-green flowers. **S. reflexum** (stone orpine) has needle-like, blue-green foliage (Zones 6–9). **S. spurium** (two-row stonecrop) produces deep pink or white flowers. Many cultivars have colorful foliage.

The large and diverse *Sedum* genus includes over 300 different species, including many that do very well in Georgia.

Growing
Sedums prefer **full sun** but tolerate partial shade. The soil should be of **average fertility** and **very well drained**. Divide in spring when needed.

Tall selections (18–24" tall and wide) include **S. 'Autumn Joy,'** with flowers that open pink or red and later fade to deep bronze (Zones 3–10), and **S. spectabile** (showy stonecrop), which blooms in white or various shades of pink.

Early-summer pruning of upright stonecrop species and hybrids encourages compact, bushy growth but can delay flowering.

Features: summer to fall flowers in yellow, yellow-green, white, red or pink; decorative fleshy foliage **Height:** 2–24" **Spread:** 10–24" or more **Hardiness:** zones 3–8

Tatarian Daisy

Aster

A. tataricus (left & right)

Tatarian daisy is a meadow and wetland plant from central Asia that has naturalized here in the American southeast. It is a big, bold plant that can really anchor a fall garden.

Growing

Tatarian daisy requires **full sun** but tolerates partial shade, albeit with fewer flowers and staking possibly required. The soil should be **moist** and **well drained**. Divide every two to three years to maintain vigor and control spread.

Tips

Plant Tatarian daisy in the middle and back of borders and in cottage gardens, or naturalize them in wild gardens.

Also called: Tatarian aster **Features:** late-summer to fall flowers in purple to lavender blue, with yellow centers **Height:** 4–7' **Spread:** 2–4' **Hardiness:** zones 3–9

Recommended

A. tataricus is an upright, clump-forming perennial that bears abundant yellow-centered, purple flowers. Individual plants grow 6–7' tall and 3–4' wide, but clumps can be wider as the plant spreads from thick rhizomes. The paddle-shaped, rough-textured, dark green leaves are 24" long and 6" wide. **'Jin-Dai'** grows 4–5' tall and 24–36" wide and bears light lavender blue flowers. It is not quite as hardy as the species.

Almost summer's last hurrah in the perennial garden, the flowers of Tatarian daisy provide food for late-season butterflies.

Toad Lily

Tricyrtis

T. hirta cultivar (above), *T. hirta* (below)

Toad lily foliage may suffer tip burn if the plant is under stress or if it gets too hot, but it won't harm the plant.

You have to get really close to appreciate toad lily's small, unusual flowers. Don't worry, though—this plant will not give you warts!

Growing

Toad lily grows well in **partial shade, light shade** or **full shade**. The soil should be **fertile, humus rich, moist** and **well drained**.

Tips

This diminutive plant is well suited to woodland gardens and shaded borders. If you have a shaded rock garden, patio or pond, toad lily is a good addition to locations where you can approach for a good look at the peculiar spotted flowers, which somewhat resemble orchids.

Recommended

T. hirta forms a clump of arching stems bearing light green leaves. It bears white flowers with purple to maroon spots in late summer and fall. Many wonderful cultivars are available.

Also called: Japanese toad lily
Features: late-summer and fall flowers in white, blue, purple or maroon, with or without spots; attractive foliage **Height:** 24–36"
Spread: 12–24" **Hardiness:** zones 4–9

Turtlehead

Chelone

*O*n late summer, when many plants have finished blooming, turtlehead flowers appear on strong stems for a wonderful late-season show.

Growing

Turtlehead grows best in **partial shade**. The soil should be **fertile, humus rich, moist** and **well drained,** but this plant tolerates clay soil and boggy conditions. Plants may become weak and floppy in too shaded a spot, so pinch the tips in spring to encourage bushy growth.

Divide the plants in spring or fall. They can be propagated from stem cuttings taken in early summer.

Tips

Turtlehead can be used in a pondside or streamside planting. It also does well in a bog garden or in any moist place where plants requiring better drainage won't grow. Along a moist, shady path, the pink blossoms are an exclamation point.

Recommended

C. glabra (*C. obliqua* 'Alba') is an upright plant that forms a dense mound of foliage. From late summer to fall, it bears white flowers tinged with light pink.

C. lyonii (pink turtlehead) is an erect plant with square stems and dark pink flowers.

As cut flowers, turtlehead blooms last 8–10 days.

Features: pink-tinged, white to dark pink flowers in late summer and fall; attractive foliage **Height:** 2–4' **Spread:** 18–30" **Hardiness:** zones 3–8

Verbena

Verbena

V. bonariensis

Verbena is an open, airy plant that will attract a plethora of butterflies to your garden.

Growing

Verbenas grow best in **full sun**. The soil should be of average **fertility** and **very well drained**. Tall verbena tolerates drought when established. Cut or pinch the plants back by one-half in mid-summer to encourage a lot of fall blooms.

During humid summers, tall verbena is prone to powdery mildew. Overall health and flowering are usually not affected, but severe outbreaks can really weaken a plant.

Tips

Use verbenas at the front or middle of beds and borders, and to add height to containers. Tall verbena self-seeds in abundance, but the seedlings are easy to keep under control. Because it is such a wispy plant in flower, tall verbena looks best when mass planted.

Recommended

V. bonariensis (tall verbena) forms a low clump of foliage from which arise tall, stiff, airy stems that bear clusters of small, purple flowers.

Also called: purpletop verbena, purpletop vervain **Features:** early- to late-summer flowers in various shades of purple; attractive habit **Height:** 3–6' **Spread:** 12–24" **Hardiness:** zones 6–9

Wild Ginger
Asarum

A. *shuttleworthii* 'Callaway' (left & right)

This species of wild ginger is native to the southeastern states. The cultivar **'Callaway'** was discovered at Callaway Gardens at Pine Mountain, north of Columbus. Make sure you spend some time visiting the wonderful gardens we have in our state.

Growing
Wild gingers need **full or partial shade**. The soil should be **moist** and **humus rich**. All *Asarum* species prefer acidic soils, such as those found in woodland conditions. Wild gingers tolerate dry conditions for a while in good shade, but prolonged drought eventually causes wilt and dieback.

Tips
Wild gingers make beautiful ground-covers for woodland sites. Use them in shady rock gardens or borders. Wild gingers are relatively easy to remove from places where they aren't welcome.

Recommended
A. *shuttleworthii* is a prostrate, mat-forming, evergreen perennial that has heart-shaped, shiny, dark green foliage with silver marbling. **'Callaway'** is a robust selection with heavy silver marbling on the foliage.

Also called: Shuttleworth ginger
Features: attractive foliage; easy to grow; unusual burgundy or green flowers
Height: 3–6" **Spread:** 12" or more
Hardiness: zones 6–9

Wild ginger flowers have a unique shape, an unusual brown-maroon color and an unpleasant, slightly fetid odor that attracts their beetle pollinators.

American Beech

Fagus

F. grandiflora (above & below)

Beechnuts provide food for a wide variety of animals, including squirrels and birds, and they were once a favorite food of the now-extinct passenger pigeon. Roasting makes beechnuts edible for humans.

The majestic beech is considered by many people to be the most beautiful of the large shade trees.

Growing

American beech grows equally well in **full sun** or **partial shade**. The soil should be of **average fertility, loamy** and **well drained,** but most well-drained soils are tolerated. American beech suffers in alkaline or poorly drained soils.

American beech doesn't like having its roots disturbed and should be transplanted only when very young. It has a tendency to produce suckers from the roots, and small trees may pop up around the mother plant; they can be carefully dug up and transplanted.

Tips

American beech makes an excellent specimen. It is used as a shade tree and in woodland gardens. American beech needs a lot of space. Not many plants like to grow within the dripline of beech trees.

Recommended

F. grandifolia (American beech) is a broad-canopied tree that is native to most of eastern North America. It grows 50–80' tall and almost as wide, but it can get much larger in ideal conditions. It retains its very smooth and elastic bark long into maturity.

Features: attractive foliage, bark and habit; fall color; fruit **Habit:** large, oval, deciduous shade tree **Height:** 50–80' **Spread:** 50–80' **Hardiness:** zones 4–9

Bald-Cypress
Taxodium

Bald-cypress is a tough, dependable tree that can grow well in a variety of conditions and climates.

Growing

Bald-cypress grows well in **full sun,** in **acidic, moist** soil, but it can adapt to most soils and conditions. Highly alkaline soil may cause the foliage to turn yellow (chlorotic). Bald-cypress develops a deep taproot but transplants fairly easily when young.

Tips

Bald-cypress can be used as a specimen tree or in a group planting. This fairly large tree looks best with plenty of space. It is ideal in a swampy or frequently wet area where few other trees would thrive.

When grown in waterlogged soil or near a water feature, bald-cypress develops gnome-like 'knees,' which are knobby roots that poke up from the water.

Recommended

T. distichum is a slender, conical tree that may grow over 100' tall in the wild. With maturity, it becomes irregular and more rounded, and the trunk becomes buttressed. In fall, the blue-green foliage turns a rusty orange before falling.

T. distichum (above & below)

People unfamiliar with bald-cypress usually expect it to be evergreen. Gasps are often heard when this deciduous conifer turns color in fall and defoliates. Plant near water to double the effect of its fall color.

Features: attractive habit, trunk and foliage; cones; fall color **Habit:** conical, deciduous, coniferous tree **Height:** 50–70'
Spread: 18–30' **Hardiness:** zones 4–9

Black Locust

Robinia

R. pseudoacacia 'Frisia' (left & right)

*I*f you need a tough tree for a disturbed or recently flooded site, black locust may be the answer.

Growing
Black locust prefers **full sun,** in **average to fertile, moist** soil, but it adapts to any soils that aren't constantly soggy. It tolerates infertile or salty soils, drought and pollution. In exposed locations, heavy wind can cause the weak branches

Black locust wood resists decay and has been used to make fence posts, mine timbers, railroad ties, insulator pins, tool handles, boxes and garden structures, such as arbors and handrails.

to break. Large pruning cuts on *Robinia* species do not heal well and should be avoided.

Tips
Black locust is best used in difficult situations where other trees fail to thrive. The small cultivars may be suitable for the home landscape.

All parts of this tree contain **poisonous** proteins. The bean-like seeds should never be eaten.

Recommended
R. pseudoacacia is an upright, suckering and self-seeding, deciduous tree. It can reach 90' in height and width in open, ideal sites. It has deeply furrowed bark and produces dangling clusters of fragrant, white flowers. Smaller, more ornamental cultivars are available.

Also called: false acacia **Features:** attractive foliage; white early-summer flowers; fast growth; spiny branches **Habit:** open, deciduous tree **Height:** 30–50' **Spread:** 20–40' **Hardiness:** zones 3–8

Bottlebrush Buckeye

Aesculus

A. parviflora (left & right)

Bottlebrush buckeye is a hardy, dependable native shrub with beautiful foliage. In late spring, it graces us with beautiful flowers. When summer's sun tilts to fall, bottlebrush buckeye turns golden yellow.

Growing

Bottlebrush buckeye grows well in **full sun** or **partial shade**. The soil should be **moist** and **well drained,** with a lot of **organic matter** mixed in. Although bottlebrush buckeye prefers an acidic soil, it can adapt to most soils but dislikes excessive drought.

Tips

Bottlebrush buckeye is useful in a small setting, where it can be used as a specimen, in shrub beds or in mixed borders. This deer-resistant plant can also be effective when mass planted in larger areas, filling unused corners or covering hard-to-mow banks.

All parts of *Aesculus* plants, especially the seeds, are **toxic**.

Recommended

A. parviflora is a spreading, mound-forming, suckering shrub that is covered with spikes of white flowers in early to mid-July. This species is not susceptible to the pests and diseases that plague its larger cousins.

Features: white late-spring to early-summer flowers; attractive foliage; spiny fruit **Habit:** spreading, deciduous shrub **Height:** 8–12' **Spread:** 8–15' **Hardiness:** zones 4–9

Bottlebrush buckeye flowers attract hummingbirds to the garden, and squirrels enjoy the seeds with no apparent harm.

Camellia

Camellia

C. japonica cultivar (above & below)

Camellias tolerate salt and pollution, making them excellent choices for coastal and urban plantings.

Growing

C. japonica prefers **light or partial shade**. *C. sasanqua* can tolerate **shade to full sun**. The soil should be **acidic to neutral**, high in **organic matter** and **well drained**. *C. japonica* prefers more acidic soil. Once established, camellias are very drought tolerant, but **protect** them from drying winds. They may also suffer extreme damage if temperatures drop below 5° F.

Plant so the base of the tree is slightly above grade and soil does not cover the base. Use organic mulch to help keep the roots cool for the first two to three years.

Tips

Camellias are evergreen plants suitable for mixed beds, borders and woodland gardens, as specimens and as container plants. The soil for container plantings should be 50% organic matter and 50% potting mix. Camellias can also have their lower branches removed to create small trees.

Recommended

Almost 300 species of camellias and thousands of cultivars exist. Check with your local nursery, garden center, or the American Camellia Society (near Fort Valley in Peach County) to see what is best for your garden.

Features: white, pink, red or (rarely) yellow flowers; attractive foliage and habit
Habit: upright to spreading shrub or small tree **Height:** 18"–20' **Spread:** 3–12'
Hardiness: zones: 7–9

Chinese Anise

Illicium

Chinese anise is an attractive, easy-to-grow, very pest-resistant shrub that grows and flowers exceptionally well in shaded conditions. In a tapestry hedge, its chartreuse foliage combines well with Florida leucothoe, privet and camellia; the colors and habits contrast beautifully.

Growing

Chinese anise grows well in **partial to full shade,** in **moist, well-drained** soil with a lot of **organic matter** mixed in. It tolerates wet soil. Provide **shelter** from both the hot afternoon sun and winter winds.

Tips

Chinese anise is very useful as a background plant in a shrub bed or mixed border. The dense foliage also makes Chinese anise useful as a screening plant. It tolerates pruning and can be used for hedges and espalier, but use hand pruners and proper pruning cuts rather than shears or a hedge trimmer. You can also train Chinese anise as a small, single-stemmed tree.

Recommended

I. anisatum is an upright, pyramidal to roundish shrub. Its shiny, medium green to yellowish green foliage has a pleasant licorice aroma when crushed or bruised. The creamy, yellowish green flowers bloom in spring, fading to white as they age. Southern natives *I. floridanum* and *I. parviflorum* are also good, sturdy shrubs.

Also called: Japanese anise
Features: creamy yellowish green flowers; attractive foliage; fruit **Habit:** broadly pyramidal, evergreen shrub **Height:** 6–10' **Spread:** 5–9'
Hardiness: zones: 7–9

I. anisatum (above & below)

Do not eat any parts of I. anisatum *or its native cousins, because all parts are highly* **toxic**.

Chinese Elm

Ulmus

U. parviflora (left & right)

The toll taken on our American elm by Dutch elm disease (DED) is saddening. Chinese elm, however, does not succumb to DED, and it is an attractive, durable, tough tree.

Growing

Chinese elm grows well in **full sun** or **partial shade**. It prefers a **moist, fertile, well-drained** soil but adapts to most soil types and conditions. It tolerates urban conditions, including salt from roadways.

Because they provide shelter and nesting sites, and many small birds eat their seeds, elms attract birds and other wildlife to your garden.

Tips

Often a large tree, Chinese elm is attractive where it has plenty of room to grow, such as on large properties and in parks. Small cultivars make attractive specimen and shade trees. Ensure the tree you get is not *U. pumila* (Siberian elm), which is an inferior tree by comparison.

Recommended

U. parviflora has a variable growth habit ranging from rounded to upright and vase-like. It has exceptionally attractive exfoliating, mottled bark and pendulous branches. It also has good drought tolerance and good disease resistance. The foliage may turn yellow to red in fall. A number of great cultivars are available, including dwarf and variegated selections.

Also called: lacebark elm **Features:** attractive habit; fall color; attractive mottled bark **Habit:** variable, rounded to vase-shaped, deciduous tree **Height:** 40–50' **Spread:** 40–50' **Hardiness:** zones 5–9

Chinese Fringe-Flower

Loropetalum

L. chinensis cultivar (above & below)

Chinese fringe-flower is an attractive spring-flowering shrub that can be used almost anywhere a large shrub is desired. The varieties with reddish purple leaves are a knockout!

Growing

Chinese fringe-flower grows best in **full sun** but does almost as well in partial or light shade. The ideal soil is **acidic, moist** and **well drained,** with a lot of **organic matter** mixed in, but Chinese fringe-flower adapts to sandy or clay soils. In the northern half of Georgia, it is best to choose a location with **shelter** from cold winter winds and to provide some **protection** when the temperature dips below zero.

Tips

Chinese fringe-flower can be used in a wide variety of shrub and mixed beds and borders. The evergreen foliage makes a nice background for other flowering plants. Chinese fringe-flower can be pruned into a small tree.

Recommended

L. chinense is a fast-growing, irregular, rounded to upright shrub with evergreen, glossy, dark green foliage and fragrant, creamy white flowers. A number of excellent selections have reddish purple leaves and showy pink flowers.

Features: white or pink spring flowers; attractive foliage; low maintenance **Habit:** low-growing, spreading, evergreen shrub **Height:** 10'
Spread: 10' **Hardiness:** zones 5–9

Common Witch-hazel

Hamamelis

H. virginiana with hydrangea (above), *H. virginiana* (below)

Providing a colorful, wonderfully aromatic fall show, these native shrubs rarely suffer any problems. They are excellent choices for use in a naturalized garden.

Growing

Common witch-hazels grow best in a **sheltered** spot with **full sun** or **light shade**. The soil should be of **average fertility, neutral to acidic, moist** and **well drained**.

In cold weather, the petals of witch-hazels roll up to protect the flowers and extend the flowering season.

Tips

Witch-hazels work well individually or in groups. Plant them as specimen plants, in shrub or mixed borders and in woodland gardens. They can be trained as small trees, which may be useful for space-limited gardens.

Recommended

H. virginiana is an attractive large, rounded shrub that spreads by suckers. The small, yellow fall flowers are often hidden by the intense fall foliage, which turns fluorescent yellow at the same time. Plant growers are now selecting and breeding plants that tend to drop their fall leaves before flowering begins. (Zones 3–8)

H. x intermedia is an upright to spreading hybrid that features fall flowers in shades of yellow to red and a similar range of fall foliage colors. (Zones 5–9)

Features: fragrant, yellow to red fall flowers; attractive foliage; fall color **Habit:** spreading, deciduous shrub or small tree **Height:** 12–20' **Spread:** 12–20' **Hardiness:** zones 3–9

Contorted Willow

Salix

S. matsudana 'Tortuosa' (left & right)

Contorted willow is truly an interesting tree. The twisted and contorted form provides an excellent show in winter, especially in silhouette. Pruning to shape guarantees this tree will be a focal point.

Growing

Contorted willow prefers **full sun** and **deep, moist, well-drained** soil. It does not do well in shallow, alkaline soil. Contorted willow is said to tolerate salt. Give young trees **shelter** from frosts below 15° F. Willows have weak wood and are subject to breakage in high winds.

Also called: corkscrew willow, dragon's claw willow **Features:** contorted and twisted stems and foliage; fall color; winter form **Habit:** upright, deciduous tree **Height:** 20–30' **Spread:** 15–20' **Hardiness:** zones 4–8

Tips

Contorted willow can be used as a single specimen or as a shade tree in a larger setting. It can be short-lived in zone 8 and warmer.

The shallow, aggressive roots may invade water and sewer pipes, and they also make it difficult to garden under the tree. Apply organic mulch out to the dripline.

Recommended

S. matsudana '**Tortuosa**' is an upright tree that has contorted and twisted stems. Bright green when young, the foliage darkens in summer and turns yellow-green in fall. 'Tortuosa' is a parent of two hybrids that better tolerate heat. '**Golden Curls**' is a hardy large shrub or small tree with arching, mildly contorted, golden-hued stems and slightly contorted foliage. SCARLET CURLS ('Scarcuzam') has scarlet red young stems and contorted foliage.

Crape Myrtle

Lagerstroemia

L. indica cultivar (above & below)

Crape myrtle is a wonderful four-season plant.

Growing

Crape myrtle performs best in **full sun** but tolerates light shade. It likes **neutral** to **slightly acidic, well-drained** soil. In alkaline or salty soil, it may show burnt leaf margins or chlorosis or both. Hot winds may also scorch the leaf margins. Ensure regular watering when young. Established plants are quite drought tolerant but do best with occasional deep watering. Do not water from overhead.

Crape myrtle may produce suckers and self-seeds readily. Once planted, it does not like to be moved.

Tips

Crape myrtle is an excellent specimen, street tree and lawn tree. Long, cool falls yield the best leaf color.

Crape myrtle can be trained as a single- or multi-stemmed tree. The lower branches and any weak stems are often removed to show off the attractive bark. Prune crape myrtle to shape only; do not 'crape murder' this plant by whacking it in half each year.

Recommended

L. indica bears showy clusters of ruffled, crepe-like flowers in white or shades of red, pink or purple all summer. The bronze-tinged, light green foliage ages to dark, glossy green in summer and turns yellow, orange or red in fall. The gray-brown bark exfoliates to reveal the pinkish bark beneath. Choose cultivars named **'Lipan,' 'Muskogee,' 'Natchez,' 'Sioux,' 'Tonto'** or **'Yuma'** to avoid powdery mildew, a common crape myrtle problem.

Features: white, pink, red or purple flowers; attractive foliage; exfoliating bark
Habit: deciduous, multi-stemmed shrub or small tree **Height:** 15–25' **Spread:** 15–25'
Hardiness: zones 7–10

Dwarf Aucuba

Aucuba

This tough plant tolerates frost, deep shade, pollution, salty, windy coastal conditions and neglect. The foliage and berries are a dynamic addition to any garden.

Growing

Aucubas grow well in **partial to full shade,** in **moderately fertile, humus-rich, moist, well-drained** soil. Selections with variegated foliage show the best leaf color in partial shade. Aucubas adapt to most soil conditions, except waterlogged, and they tolerate urban pollution.

Tips

Dwarf aucuba can be used in deeply shaded locations where no other plants will grow, such as under the canopy of larger trees. It can also be used as a specimen, in a large planter and as a hedge or screen.

Generally, both male and female plants must be present for the females to set fruit (which is inedible).

Recommended

A. japonica 'Nana' is a compact plant with erect stems, a neatly rounded habit and glossy, green leaves. Half the size of the species, it grows 3–4' tall and wide. Female plants develop red berries in fall. Held above the foliage, the fruit is highly visible. Many other cultivars of *A. japonica,* usually developed for their variegated foliage, are available.

A. japonica cultivar (above & below)

Also called: dwarf Japanese aucuba
Features: attractive foliage; fruit; adaptability
Habit: bushy, rounded, evergreen shrub
Height: 3–4' **Spread:** 3–4'
Hardiness: zones 7–10

Elaeagnus

Elaeagnus

E. pungens cultivar (above & below)

Elaeagnus is another tough-as-nails shrub that withstands drought, salty conditions and pollution. It grows so well in Georgia that some people consider it a weed.

Growing

Grow elaeagnus in **full sun** or **partial shade**. It prefers a **well-drained, sandy loam** of **average to high fertility** but can adapt to poor, heavy clay soil, because it can 'fix' nitrogen from the air. A tolerance for salty and dry conditions makes it useful for plantings along highways and other salted roads. Elaeagnus

requires little if any watering after the second year.

Tips

This tough plant works well in shrub or mixed borders and in hedges or screens. It is also useful for erosion control and soil stabilization.

Recommended

E. pungens is a spiny, evergreen shrub that is resistant to deer and rabbits, and spreads by suckers. The foliage is dark silvery green on top and silvery white beneath. Fragrant, tiny, silvery white flowers are produced in fall. The subsequent fruit, which begins brown and ripens to red, attracts wildlife. **'Variegata'** has yellow leaf margins.

Also called: thorny elaeagnus
Features: fragrant flowers; summer foliage; easy to grow **Habit:** large, sprawling, evergreen shrub with arching canes **Height:** 10–15'
Spread: 10–15' **Hardiness:** zones 7–10

False Cypress
Chamaecyparis

The best false cypress for use in Georgia is *C. thyoides*. This native plant excels in conditions that resemble its normal habitat of stream banks, lowlands and boggy areas.

Growing

False cypresses prefer **full sun**. The soil should be **fertile, neutral to acidic** and **moist**; *C. thyoides* grows well in **wet** soils. Alkaline soils are tolerated. In shaded areas, growth may be sparse or thin.

Tips

Use this tree as a specimen or for hedging and screening. The dwarf and slow-growing cultivars are used in borders and rock gardens or as bonsai. This conifer peaks while deciduous shrubs are dormant, making it a perfect companion plant.

Recommended

C. thyoides is a narrow, pyramidal to columnar tree with blue-green to green sprays of needle-like foliage. The foliage may turn bronze to brown during the cold winter months. A large number of cultivars are available, ranging from compact (under 4') and globe-shaped to tall and cone-like, with foliage ranging from green to blue-green to bright gold.

C. thyoides 'Heather Bun' (above), *C. thyoides* (below)

The oils in false cypress foliage may irritate sensitive skin.

Also called: Atlantic white cedar
Features: attractive foliage and habit; cones
Habit: narrow, pyramidal, evergreen tree or shrub **Height:** 40–50' (much larger in the wild)
Spread: 10–20' **Hardiness:** zones 4–8

Flame Azalea

Rhododendron

R. calendulaceum (left & right)

Flame azalea is a native shrub that ignites our gardens with an explosion of color in spring.

Growing

Flame azalea prefers **partial or light shade,** with **shelter** from the hot afternoon sun. The soil should be **fertile, humus rich, acidic, moist** and **very well drained,** although this species tolerates some drought. **Shelter** from strong winds is preferable. Azaleas and rhododendrons are sensitive to high pH, salinity and winter injury.

Tips

Use flame azalea in shrub or mixed borders, in a woodland garden, as a specimen plant, in group plantings, in hedges or informal barriers, and in planters on a shady patio or balcony. Flame azalea is an excellent plant for naturalizing.

Recommended

R. calendulaceum is an upright to rounded, deciduous shrub with medium green foliage that turns yellow to red in fall. It bears clusters of unscented, colorful flowers in shades of red, orange, yellow, apricot, salmon, pink or gold. This plant is slow to establish. Cultivars are available.

Although we list only one species here, a huge number of different rhododendron and azalea species and cultivars exist. Check with your local nurseries and specialty growers to help you find the rhododendron or azalea that will work best for you.

Azaleas and rhododendrons have fine, web-like roots that grow close to the soil surface and need excellent drainage to avoid problems. Plant shallowly in our Georgia soils.

Features: mid- to late-spring flowers; attractive foliage **Habit:** rounded, deciduous shrub **Height:** 6–10' **Spread:** 6–10' **Hardiness:** zones 5–8

Florida Leucothoe

Agarista

Florida leucothoe is a useful native shrub that excels in shady, moist locations and remains attractive year-round. As a bonus, the honey-scented flowers attract bees and butterflies.

Growing

Florida leucothoe grows well in **light**, **partial** or **full shade**. The soil should be **fertile, acidic, humus rich, moist** and on the **cool** side, and this plant tolerates wet soils. For optimum performance, ensure **shelter** from the direct afternoon sun.

Tips

Florida leucothoe makes an excellent foliage plant. Include it in woodland gardens and shaded borders. Use Florida leucothoe with rhododendrons, as a background for azaleas or as an understory plant.

Recommended

A. populifolia (*Leucothoe populifolia*) is a dense, multi-stemmed shrub that spreads by suckers. It has lax, arching stems and evergreen, glossy, green foliage that is pink to red-tinged when new. Fragrant, urn-shaped, creamy white flowers bloom from mid- to late spring.

A. populifolia (above & below)

*Eating the **highly toxic** leaves of Florida leucothoe results in severe illness or death.*

Also called: pipestem, fetter-bush, Florida hobblebush **Features:** white spring flowers; attractive foliage **Habit:** upright, bushy, evergreen shrub with arching stems **Height:** 8–12' **Spread:** 6–10' **Hardiness:** zones 7–9

Flowering Cherry

Prunus

P. subhirtella 'Pendula Rosea' (above)

Flowering cherries are beautiful and uplifting visions of spring that chase away the winter blahs.

Growing

These trees prefer **full sun**. The soil should be of **average fertility, moist** and **well drained**. Shallow roots emerging from the lawn indicate insufficient water; flowering cherries need plenty of water when the temperature exceeds 90° F.

Tips

Prunus species make beautiful specimen plants for almost any garden. Small species and cultivars can also be included in borders or grouped to form informal hedges or barriers.

Pest problems can afflict many of the cherries, and they can be rather short-lived. If you plant a susceptible species, enjoy it while it thrives, but be prepared to replace it.

Recommended

A plethora of wonderful *Prunus* plants are available. Check with your local nursery or garden center for other possible selections.

P. x *incam* '**Okame**' is an upright to rounded tree that bears early, carmine pink flowers. *P.* '**Dream Catcher**' is an upright, vase-shaped tree with a high tolerance for insects and diseases. It bears large, medium pink flowers.

P. x *yedoensis* (Yoshino cherry) is a spreading tree with arching branches and white flowers.

Features: pink or white early-spring to early-summer flowers; fruit; attractive bark; yellow to red fall foliage **Habit:** upright, rounded, spreading or weeping, deciduous tree or shrub **Height:** 20–30' **Spread:** 15–30' **Hardiness:** zones 5–8

Gardenia
Gardenia

No Southern garden should be without gardenia's intoxicating aroma.

Growing

Gardenia grows well in **full sun** or **light shade,** in **slightly acidic, well-drained** soil. Although a plant killed to the ground will regenerate from the roots, it is best to choose a location with **shelter** from cold winter winds. Draping a sheet over the entire plant or putting a large cardboard box over a young shrub provides protection from cold.

Water high in salts may burn the foliage; never use water that has been run through a water softener. Regularly leach the excess salts from the soil.

Gardenia has shallow roots and does not compete well in a crowded situation. Avoid cultivating around the plant; use organic mulch instead.

Tips

Gardenia grows very well in containers and raised beds. It also produces unusual hedges, espaliers and specimen plants.

Recommended

G. jasminoides is an evergreen shrub that bears fragrant, cream to white flowers from summer to fall. A number of good cultivars are available in varying plant and leaf sizes, with single or double flowers. Cold hardiness may be a factor in zone 7. In the northern half of our state, ensure you select plants that are able to handle the colder conditions.

G. jasminoides (above & below)

Gardenia's glossy, dark green foliage is quite showy.

Also called: Cape jasmine **Features:** intensely fragrant flowers; foliage **Habit:** upright to rounded, evergreen tree or shrub **Height:** 4–6' **Spread:** 4–8' **Hardiness:** zones 8–11

Glossy Abelia
Abelia

A. x *grandiflora* (above & below)

Glossy abelia is blessed with attractive foliage, great flowers and interesting bark. This striking, easy-to-grow shrub can attract butterflies, praying mantises and hummingbirds to your garden.

Growing

Glossy abelia prefers **full sun** but tolerates partial shade. The soil should be **slightly acidic, fertile, moist** and **well drained**, although glossy abelia is extremely drought tolerant once established. Choose a spot with **shelter** from cold, drying winds.

Tips

Glossy abelia is good for both formal and informal gardens and hedges, and it is attractive individually or in groups. It can be used in shrub or mixed borders. Clematis vines weave beautifully through glossy abelia.

In mild areas, glossy abelia is evergreen; in cool areas, it is semi-evergreen. If the leaves and stems are severely damaged by winter cold, the plant will grow back from the roots, which are mostly cold hardy.

Recommended

A. **x** *grandiflora* produces white or pale pink flowers sporadically all summer. The glossy, dark green foliage turns red or bronze in fall, persisting through winter in mild areas. In colder areas, the leaves drop, revealing the attractive exfoliating stems. Variegated and compact cultivars are available.

Features: white or pink flowers; attractive foliage and stems **Habit:** large, rounded, evergreen or semi-evergreen shrub with arching stems **Height:** 4–8' **Spread:** 4–8' **Hardiness:** zones 6–9

Golden Rain Tree

Koelreuteria

K. paniculata (above & below)

Beautiful, tough and adaptable, golden rain tree excels in our Southern gardens. It is one of the few trees with yellow flowers and one of the few trees to flower in summer.

Growing

Golden rain tree grows best in **full sun**. The soil should be **average to fertile, moist** and **well drained**. This tree tolerates heat, drought, wind and polluted air. It is also pH adaptable.

Tips

Golden rain tree makes an excellent shade or specimen tree for small properties. Its ability to adapt to a wide range of soils makes it useful in many situations. The fruit can be messy but does not stain patios or decks. Golden rain tree looks great when underplanted with blue mophead hydrangeas.

Recommended

K. paniculata is an attractive rounded, spreading tree that grows 30–40' tall, with an equal or greater width. It bears long clusters of small, yellow flowers. The attractive leaves are somewhat lacy in appearance, and they sometimes turn bright yellow in fall. **'Fastigiata'** is an upright, columnar tree that grows 25' tall and 6' wide.

Features: attractive habit and foliage; mid-summer flowers **Habit:** rounded, spreading, deciduous tree **Height:** 25–40' **Spread:** 6–40' or more **Hardiness:** zones 6–8

Grancy Gray-Beard

Chionanthus

C. virginicus (above & below)

Grancy gray-beard is a beautiful native shrub that can adapt to a wide range of growing conditions. Early summer sees it densely covered in silky, honey-scented flowers that shimmer in the breeze.

Growing

Grancy gray-beard prefers **full sun**. It does best in soil that is **fertile, acidic, moist** and **well drained** but adapts to most soil conditions.

Tips

Grancy gray-beard works well as a specimen plant, as part of a border or beside a water feature. It flowers in early age.

The fruit of grancy gray-beard attracts birds. Both male and female flowers are needed for fruit to form. They are usually borne on separate plants, but sometimes both sexes appear on the same plant.

Recommended

C. virginicus is a spreading, small tree or large shrub that bears fragrant, drooping, white flowers.

Also called: white fringe tree **Features:** white early-summer flowers; attractive bark and habit **Habit:** rounded or spreading, deciduous, large shrub or small tree **Height:** 10–25' **Spread:** 10–25' **Hardiness:** zones 4–8

Heavenly Bamboo

Nandina

N. domestica (above), *N. domestica* 'Compacta' (below)

N amed for the similarity of its foliage to bamboo foliage, heavenly bamboo is not a relative of true bamboo.

Growing

Heavenly bamboo prefers **full sun** or **partial shade,** in **humus-rich, moist, well-drained** soil. It is prone to chlorosis when planted in alkaline soils. It prefers regular water but can tolerate drier conditions. Shrubs in full sun that experience some frost produce the best fall and winter color.

Tips

Use heavenly bamboo in shrub borders, as a background plant and for informal hedges or screens. It is a great plant for containers. Mass planting ensures a good quantity of the shiny, bright red berries.

Also called: sacred bamboo, common nandina
Features: white late-spring to early-summer flowers; fruit; decorative foliage; tough; long-lived **Habit:** upright to rounded, evergreen or semi-evergreen shrub **Height:** 18"–8'
Spread: 18"–5' **Hardiness:** zones 7–9

Recommended

N. domestica produces clumps of thin, upright, lightly branched stems and fine textured foliage. It grows 6–8' tall and spreads 3–5' wide, spreading slowly by suckering. It bears large, loose clusters of small, white flowers followed by persistent, spherical fruit. Initially tinged bronze to red, the foliage becomes light to medium green in summer, with many varieties turning red to reddish purple in fall and winter. Many colorful, compact and dwarf cultivars are available.

Holly
Ilex

I. opaca hybrid (left), *I. cornuta* 'Carissa' (right)

Hollies are durable shrubs and trees that vary greatly in shape and size. When given conditions they like, they thrive for years.

Growing
These plants prefer **full sun** but tolerate partial shade. The soil should be of **average to high fertility, humus rich** and **moist**. Hollies perform best in acidic soil with a pH of 6.5 or lower. **Shelter** hollies from winter wind to help prevent the evergreen leaves from drying out. Apply a summer mulch to keep the roots cool and moist.

Many hollies attract birds that use the plants for food and shelter.

Tips
Hollies can be used in groups, in woodland gardens and in shrub and mixed borders. Many can also be shaped into hedges, topiary and espalier with hand pruners.

Recommended
The following holly species do very well in Georgia gardens. Many cultivars of different sizes and leaf shapes are available for each of the species. Check with your local nursery or garden center to see what is available. *I. cornuta* (Chinese holly), *I. glabra* (inkberry) and *I. vomitoria* (yaupon) are evergreen shrubs. *I. opaca* (American holly) is a large, evergreen tree. *I. verticillata* (winterberry) is a deciduous species grown for its explosion of red, orange or yellow fruit that persists past fall.

Features: decorative glossy, often-spiny foliage; fruit; attractive habit **Habit:** erect or spreading, evergreen or deciduous shrub or tree **Height:** 3–20' for shrub species; 40–50' for tree species **Spread:** 3–15' for shrub species; 30–40' for tree species **Hardiness:** zones 3–9

Hydrangea
Hydrangea

Hydrangeas have many attractive qualities, including showy flowers and glossy, green leaves, some of which turn beautiful colors in fall.

Growing

Hydrangeas grow well in **full sun** or **partial shade,** and some species tolerate full shade. Providing some shade reduces leaf and flower scorch in hot regions. The soil should be of **average to high fertility, humus rich, moist** and **well drained**.

Tips

Hydrangeas come in many forms and have many landscape uses. They can be included in shrub or mixed borders, used as specimens or informal barriers, or planted in groups.

Recommended

Hundreds of great cultivars and hybrids are available. The following hydrangeas perform well in Southern gardens.

H. arborescens (smooth hydrangea) is a rounded shrub that spreads by suckers. It flowers well even in shade. *H. macrophylla* (bigleaf hydrangea) is a rounded or mounding shrub. Many cultivars are available. *H. paniculata* (panicle hydrangea) is a large, spreading to upright shrub or small tree. *H. quercifolia* (oakleaf hydrangea) is a mound-forming native shrub that spreads by suckers. It has attractive exfoliating bark and large, oak-like leaves.

H. quercifolia (above), *H. macrophylla* (below)

Traces of cyanide are found in the leaves and buds of some hydrangeas. Wash your hands well after handling these plants. Avoid burning the clippings, because the smoke can be **toxic***.*

Features: showy flowers; attractive habit, foliage and bark **Habit:** mounding or spreading, deciduous shrub or tree **Height:** 3–12'
Spread: 2–12' **Hardiness:** zones 3–8

Japanese Cryptomeria
Cryptomeria

Japanese cryptomeria is a graceful, refined tree that is becoming quite popular in United Stated gardens.

Growing
Japanese cryptomeria prefers partial to light shade but will tolerate **full sun**. The soil should be **acidic, fertile, moist** and **very well drained,** with a lot of **organic matter** mixed in. Provide **shelter** from high wind and cold, drying winter winds.

Tips
Japanese cryptomeria is used as a specimen plant where space allows. It also makes an effective screen. The small cultivars can be included in mixed beds and shrub beds.

Recommended
C. japonica is a large, fast-growing, pyramidal to columnar tree with needle-like, bright green to blue-green leaves and fibrous, red-brown bark that peels off in long strips. The foliage often turns bronze to brown in winter, becoming green again in spring. A number of wonderful cultivars are available, ranging down to truly dwarf sizes and offering variable forms and bright yellow to dark green foliage.

Japanese cryptomeria has been used for centuries in Japan as an ornamental tree and for high quality, rot-resistant lumber. In its native habitat, it can grow up to 180' tall, with a 12' trunk diameter.

C. japonica 'Black Dragon' (above)
C. japonica 'Radicans' (below)

Also called: Japanese cedar **Features:** graceful form; attractive foliage and bark
Habit: pyramidal to columnar, evergreen tree
Height: 1–60' **Spread:** 1–30'
Hardiness: zones 6–9

Japanese Kerria

Kerria

K. japonica 'Pleniflora' (above & below)

Japanese kerria works very well as a rambling understory shrub in a woodland garden or as a pruned specimen in a shrub border. The bright yellow, spring-blooming flowers, yellow fall foliage and distinctive arching, yellow-green to bright green stems make Japanese kerria an excellent addition to a garden.

Growing

Japanese kerria prefers **light, partial or full shade,** but it tolerates full sun. The soil should be of **average fertility** and **well drained.** Soil that is too fertile reduces flower production.

Tips

Try using Japanese kerria in group plantings, woodland gardens and shrub or mixed borders.

Recommended

K. japonica grows 3–6' tall and spreads up to 10', bearing yellow single flowers for a long period from late winter through early spring. Sporadic flowers may appear in summer. Cultivars are available with variegated foliage, double flowers and pale or white flowers. **'Pleniflora'** grows looser and taller than the species and has interesting ball-shaped, fully double blooms.

Features: late-winter to early-spring flowers in yellow or white; attractive habit **Habit:** suckering, mounding, deciduous shrub **Height:** 3–10' **Spread:** 4–10' **Hardiness:** zones 4–8

Japanese Kerria's yellow-green to bright green stems add interest to a winter landscape.

Kousa Dogwood

Cornus

Kousa dogwood is more dependable and disease resistant than many other dogwood species. The distinctly tiered branches and spreading crown of Kousa dogwood add classic beauty to your garden.

Growing

Kousa dogwood grows equally well in **full sun, light shade** or **partial shade**. The soil should be of **average to high fertility,** high in **organic matter, neutral** or **slightly acidic** and **well drained**.

Tips

Kousa dogwood makes a wonderful specimen and is small enough to include in most gardens. Use it along the edge of a woodland garden, in a shrub or mixed border, or near a pond, water feature or patio.

Recommended

C. kousa is grown for its flowers, fruit, fall color and interesting bark. It is normally a large, multi-stemmed shrub, but it can be trained as a single-stemmed tree. The white-bracted flowers are followed by edible, raspberry-like, bright red fruit. The foliage turns yellow or red in fall. The bark exfoliates to form a colorful patchwork of gray, tan and brown. Cultivars are available.

C. kousa (above), *C. kousa* var. *chinensis* (below)

Kousa dogwood is more resistant to leaf blight and other problems than is C. florida *(eastern dogwood, flowering dogwood).*

Features: late-spring to early-summer flowers; fall color; exfoliating bark; fruit **Habit:** deciduous, large shrub or small tree **Height:** 20–30' **Spread:** 20–30' **Hardiness:** zones 5–8

Leatherleaf Mahonia

Mahonia

Leatherleaf mahonia is a slow-growing, trouble-free shrub that is excellent for attracting birds to your garden. When the grape-like, blue fruits are ripe, the birds devour them with gusto.

Growing

Leatherleaf mahonia prefers **light or partial shade;** full shade may reduce flower production, and full sun is tolerated in the cooler, more northerly parts of Georgia, although **protection** from the hot afternoon sun is preferred. The soil should be **neutral to slightly acidic, humus rich, moist** and **well drained**. Provide **shelter** from cold, drying winter winds.

Tips

Leatherleaf mahonia looks great in groups of three or more. Use it in mixed or shrub borders, as a specimen and in woodland gardens. It truly excels as a transition plant between a woodland garden and a more formal garden.

Recommended

M. bealei is an open, upright shrub. Its mildly fragrant, lemon yellow flowers are followed by clusters of light blue berries. The spiny-edged foliage is dull blue-green and very leathery.

M. bealei (above & below)

Features: fragrant, yellow late-winter to spring flowers; late-spring to early-summer fruit; leathery foliage **Habit:** upright, evergreen shrub **Height:** 6–12' **Spread:** 6–10' **Hardiness:** zones 6–9

The juicy berries of leatherleaf mahonia are edible but somewhat tart. They can be eaten fresh or used to make jellies, juices or wine—if you get to them before the birds do.

Magnolia
Magnolia

M. grandiflora (above), M. grandiflora hybrid (below)

Magnolias are magnificent, versatile plants that bear fragrant, stunningly beautiful flowers. If you have the space, seriously consider planting one or more of these handsome, stately trees.

Growing

Magnolias grow well in **full sun** or **partial shade**. The soil should be **fertile, humus rich, acidic, moist** and **well drained**. A summer mulch helps keep the roots cool and the soil moist.

Tips

Large selections are best used as specimen trees in large spaces. Small cultivars can be used as specimens, screens and hedges. Magnolias are not meant to have their lower branches removed, and they do look best branched to the ground.

Magnolias cast dense shade, and the shallow roots compete very well for nutrients and water, making it difficult to grow anything underneath them.

Recommended

M. grandiflora (southern magnolia, evergreen magnolia, bull bay) is a large, dense, broad, pyramidal to rounded native tree with large, shiny, evergreen leaves. Its spectacular, fragrant blooms have inspired poets and artists for generations. Narrowly columnar forms and shrubby, dwarf forms are available.

Many other species, hybrids and cultivars are available, in a range of sizes and with differing flowering times and flower colors. Check with your local nursery or garden center for other available magnolias.

Features: fragrant flowers; fruit; attractive foliage, habit and bark **Habit:** large, broadly pyramidal to rounded tree **Height:** 20–80' **Spread:** 10–50' **Hardiness:** zones 7–9

Maple
Acer

A. palmatum var. *atropurpureum* cultivar (above & below)

Maples are attractive year-round, with delicate flowers in spring, beautiful foliage and hanging samaras (winged fruit) in summer, vibrant leaf color in fall and interesting bark and branch structures in winter.

Growing

Plant *A. palmatum* in **partial, light or full shade,** ensuring shade from the hot afternoon sun and **shelter** from drying winds. Grow *A. rubrum* in **full sun.** The soil should be **fertile,** high in **organic matter, moist** and **well drained.**

Tips

Use maples as specimen, shade or street trees, as large elements in shrub or mixed borders and for hedges. *A. palmatum* is useful as an understory plant bordering wooded areas, and it can be grown in containers on patios or terraces.

Features: decorative foliage, bark and form; samaras; fall color; greenish flowers
Habit: deciduous, single- or multi-stemmed tree or large shrub **Height:** 3–60'
Spread: 5–60' **Hardiness:** zones 4–8

Recommended

A. palmatum (Japanese maple) generally grows 15–25' tall, with an equal or greater spread, although many cultivars and varieties are much smaller. Because it leafs out early in spring, this tree can be badly damaged or killed by a late-spring frost. Selections are available with purple to red foliage and dissected foliage. (Zones 5–8)

A. rubrum (red maple) is a single- or multi-stemmed tree, pyramidal when young but becoming more rounded as it matures. It grows 40–60' tall, with a variable spread of 20–60'. Choose locally bred trees–they perform better than non-locally grown varieties. The fall foliage color varies from bright yellow to orange or red.

Oak

Quercus

Q. phellos (above), Q. virginiana (below)

Acorns are generally not edible, but some kinds can be eaten after the bitter tannins have been leached out.

There are many great oaks for Georgia gardens. We suggest a tour of the University of Georgia campus, where many magnificent oak species (as well as hundreds of other great trees and shrubs hardy in Georgia) are displayed.

Growing

Oaks grow well in **full sun,** in **fertile, slightly acidic, moist, well-drained** soil. These trees can be difficult to establish; transplant them only when they are young. Oaks grow fast for their first ten years of life and then slow down.

Tips

Oaks are large trees that are best as specimens or for groves in parks and large gardens. Do not disturb the ground around the base of an oak; these trees are very sensitive to changes in grade.

Recommended

Here are some of the best large oaks. *Q. falcata* (southern red oak) grows 70–80' tall and wide. *Q. georgiana* (Georgia oak) reaches 15–30' tall and wide. *Q. lyrata* (overcup oak) grows 40–60' tall and wide. *Q. michauxii* (swamp chestnut oak) achieves 70–80' in height and spread. *Q. nuttallii* (Nuttall oak) grows 40–60' tall and wide. *Q. phellos* (willow oak) can reach 40–60' tall and wide. *Q. prinus* (chestnut oak) reaches 60–70' in height and width. *Q. virginiana* (live oak) is our official state tree; it grows 40–80' tall and 60–100' wide.

Features: summer and fall foliage; attractive bark; acorns **Habit:** large, rounded, spreading, deciduous tree **Height:** 15–80' **Spread:** 15–100' **Hardiness:** zones 4–9

Pine
Pinus

P. palustris (left), *P. taeda* (right)

The northern edge of our state marks the southern hardiness boundary for many species of pines. Fortunately, there are some good, picturesque pines for Georgia.

Growing

Pines grow best in **full sun,** but *P. taeda* adapts to **partial shade.** Pines adapt to most **well-drained** soils but do not tolerate polluted urban conditions.

Tips

Pines can be used as specimen trees, as screens or to create windbreaks. They look good when given the space to develop their interesting branching habits.

Recommended

P. echinata (shortleaf pine, yellow pine) is dense and pyramidal when young, developing into a tall tree with a branchless trunk topped by a small, pyramidal crown. It grows 50–80' tall and 20–30' wide. (Zones 6–9)

P. palustris (longleaf pine, southern yellow pine) is a very interesting species with needles 8–18" long and huge cones up to 10" long. It grows 60–70' tall and 20–25' wide. When young, it looks like a clump of grass. (Zones 7–10)

P. taeda (loblolly pine) is pyramidal when young, developing into a tall tree with a branchless trunk and topped by a rounded crown with horizontal branches. It grows 50–80' tall and 30–40' wide. (Zones 6–9)

Features: attractive foliage, bark and habit; cones; fast growth **Habit:** upright, evergreen tree **Height:** 50–80' **Spread:** 20–40'
Hardiness: zones 6–10

Redbud

Cercis

This outstanding native plant is truly a welcome sight in spring. The intense, deep magenta buds open to pink flowers that cover the long, thin branches in clouds of color. Redbud is one of Georgia's best understory trees.

Growing

Redbud grows well in **full sun, partial shade** or **light shade**; it appreciates some **protection** from the hottest afternoon sun. The soil should be a **fertile, deep loam** that is **moist** and **well drained**. This plant has tender roots and does not like being transplanted.

Tips

Redbud can be used as a specimen tree, in a shrub or mixed border and in a woodland garden. A locally grown redbud will perform best.

Recommended

C. canadensis (eastern redbud) is a spreading, multi-stemmed tree that bears red, purple or pink flowers. The young foliage is bronze, fading to green over summer and turning bright yellow in fall. Many beautiful cultivars are available. **'Alba'** (var. *alba*) has white flowers. **'Forest Pansy'** has purple or pink flowers and dark reddish purple foliage that fades to green over summer.

C. canadensis (above & below)

Features: red, purple, pink or white spring flowers; seedpods; fall color **Habit:** rounded or spreading, multi-stemmed, deciduous tree or shrub **Height:** 20–30' **Spread:** 25–35' **Hardiness:** zones 4–9

River Birch

Betula

When it comes to showy bark, the river birch is unmatched. Its attractive, peeling bark adds a whole new dimension to the garden.

Growing

River birch grows well in **full sun, partial shade** or **light shade,** in **moist, fairly well-drained, neutral to slightly acidic** soil of **average fertility**. River birch tolerates occasional flooding and wet soils.

Tips

Birch trees are often used as specimens. Their small leaves and open canopy provide light shade that allows perennials, annuals and lawns to flourish below. If you have enough space, birches look attractive when grown in groups near natural or artificial water features.

Recommended

B. nigra (river birch, black birch, red birch) has shaggy, cinnamon brown bark that flakes off in sheets when the tree is young, but the bark thickens and becomes more ridged as the tree matures. This species is resistant to pests and diseases. DURA-HEAT ('BNMTF'), discovered in Georgia, can really handle our heat. The densely packed, small, glossy, dark green leaves resist leaf spot and turn a nice yellow in fall. HERITAGE ('Cully') is a vigorous grower that resists leaf spot and heat stress. It has larger, glossier leaves than the species. The bark begins peeling when the tree is quite young.

B. nigra (above & below)

River birch is one of Georgia's showiest trees in winter.

Features: attractive foliage and bark; fall color; winter and spring catkins **Habit:** open, single or multi-stemmed, deciduous tree **Height:** 40–70' **Spread:** 30–50' **Hardiness:** zones 3–9

Sassafras

Sassafras

S. *albidum* (above & below)

As well as providing one of the principal original flavorings for root beer, sassafras has also contributed to humanity a wide range of herbal remedies and teas.

Growing

Sassafras grows well in **full sun, partial shade** or **light shade**. The soil should be of **average fertility, acidic, humus rich, moist** and **well drained**. To avoid disturbing the deep taproot, plant this tree in its permanent location when it is young.

Tips

Sassafras can be used as a specimen in a woodland garden, near a water feature or along a roadside. It is attractive in naturalized plantings, but it isn't a strong competitor and may eventually be overcome by other plants.

Recommended

S. albidum is a medium to large, irregular, suckering tree. If left in place, the suckers form a dense colony. The aromatic leaves may be unlobed or have two or three lobes, with different leaf types present on the same plant. The leaves turn bright red in fall. Male and female flowers are borne on separate plants in spring. Female plants bear fruit that ripens to dark blue and is a favorite food of birds.

Features: aromatic foliage; fall color; attractive habit and bark **Habit:** irregular to pyramidal, suckering, deciduous tree **Height:** 30–60' **Spread:** 25–40' **Hardiness:** zones 4–9

Spreading Plum Yew

Cephalotaxus

C. harringtonia 'Prostrata' (above), *C. harringtonia* cultivar (below)

This slow-growing, yew-like shrub offers all of the wonderful qualities of yews (*Taxus* species), but it can tolerate our Southern heat much better.

Growing

Spreading plum yew grows well in **partial, light or full shade** but tolerates full sun in cool parts of Georgia. The soil should be **sandy, moist, well drained** and **slightly acidic**. Established plants tolerate drought. Choose a location that provides **shelter** from drying winds.

Tips

Spreading plum yew is excellent for mass planting, and it thrives in foundation plantings. This plant tolerates hard pruning, making it ideal for low hedging material. It mixes well into borders and beds. Spreading plum yew grows slowly but is worth the wait.

Recommended

C. harringtonia 'Prostrata' is a variable, low-growing and spreading, coniferous, evergreen shrub with upright to arching branches. It bears sharply pointed, slightly curved, dark green needles that have two lighter colored bands on the undersides. The needles arise from the twigs in two rows, forming a flattened V-shape. The plum-like fruit is fleshy, greenish to reddish brown and edible, as is the seed contained within.

Features: evergreen foliage; fruit; attractive habit **Habit:** low-growing to sprawling, evergreen shrub **Height:** 18–36" **Spread:** 3–6' **Hardiness:** zones 6–9

Sweetbox

Sarcococca

S. *hookeriana* var. *humilis* (above & below)

Sweetbox is an ideal plant for garden areas that the sun can't reach directly but do receive some light.

Growing

Sweetbox grows well in **partial, light or full shade**. The soil should be of **average fertility, humus rich, moist** and **well drained**. Once established, this plant tolerates drought.

Tips

Sweetbox can be used in shady borders, as a groundcover, in woodland gardens

and for low hedges. It can also be combined with plants in the heather family, such as rhododendrons.

If sweetbox is under the eaves of a house or somewhere else where winter rains do not wash off the foliage, it is a good idea to give it a good cleaning after the blooming cycle.

Recommended

S. hookeriana is a dense, bushy, suckering shrub that grows 4–6' tall, with an equal or greater spread. The tiny, white blooms, which have a giant fragrance, appear in late winter or early spring. Some dark blue fruits may form if the spent flowers are not removed. **Var. *humilis*** is a dwarf, clump-forming shrub that grows 18–24" tall and spreads 6–8' or wider with age. It bears fragrant, white flowers tinged with pink.

Also called: Himalayan sarcococca
Features: white early-spring flowers; fruit; attractive foliage **Habit:** dense, suckering, evergreen shrub **Height:** 18"–6'
Spread: 4–8' **Hardiness:** zones 6–8

Sweet Shrub
Calycanthus

C. floridus (above & below)

Plant sweet shrub near pathways or entryways so that passersby can appreciate the fragrance of the blooms.

Growing

Sweet shrub grows well in **full sun to full shade,** in **moist, fertile** soil with a lot of **organic matter.** Ensure you provide regular water. Prune only to remove dead, diseased or damaged branches.

Tips

Sweet shrub is effective as a background shrub in a mixed or shrub bed, or as screening. It will form a thicket if left unattended.

Sweet shrub is very easy to grow from seed or by layering branches.

Recommended

C. floridus is a vigorous, deciduous shrub that spreads by suckers. In late spring and early summer, it produces brown-tipped, deep red flowers that resemble small water lilies and have a sweet aroma. The lush, dark green leaves have a camphor-like odor when bruised or crushed; they turn yellow in fall. The wood and bark are also aromatic. The seeds of sweet shrub are **poisonous** and should not be eaten. **'Athens'** is consistently fragrant and bears ivory blossoms.

Also called: spicebush, Carolina allspice, pineapple shrub, strawberry bush **Features:** red or ivory flowers; fragrance; handsome foliage; easy to grow **Habit:** rounded to irregular, multi-stemmed shrub **Height:** 5–8' **Spread:** 5–8' **Hardiness:** zones 5–9

Viburnum

Viburnum

V. x burkwoodii (above & below)

Viburnum is a large genus of excellent garden plants. They are easy to grow, quite tough and attractive in any garden.

Viburnums look great in the shade of evergreen trees. Their richly textured foliage complements shrubs and perennials that bloom in late spring.

Growing

Viburnums grow well in **full sun, partial shade** or **light shade**. The soil should be of **average fertility, slightly acidic, moist** and **well drained**.

Tips

Viburnums can be used in borders and woodland gardens. They are a good choice for plantings near patios, decks and swimming pools.

Recommended

Many viburnum species, hybrids and cultivars of varying hardiness are available. The following are two of the best viburnums for Georgia gardens.

V.* x *burkwoodii (Burkwood viburnum) is an upright to rounded, deciduous to semi-evergreen shrub. In most of Georgia, the leaves remain green all year. It grows 6–10' tall and spreads 5–8'. Clusters of fragrant, pinkish white flowers appear in mid- to late spring. The subsequent red fruit ripens to black. (Zones 4–8)

V. macrocephalum (Chinese snowball viburnum) is a large, rounded, multi-stemmed shrub, 12–15' tall and wide, with semi-evergreen, dark green foliage. The large 6–8" diameter clusters of sterile, showy white spring flowers resemble those of hydrangea. (Zones 6–9)

Features: possibly fragrant, white to pinkish flowers; attractive foliage and habit
Habit: bushy or spreading, semi-evergreen or deciduous shrub **Height:** 6–15'
Spread: 5–15' **Hardiness:** zones 4–9

Virginia Sweetspire

Itea

Virginia sweetspire is val-ued for the fragrance that emanates from its showy, elon-gated bottlebrush flower clus-ters. Vibrant fall color is another reason to use sweetspire.

Growing

Virginia sweetspire grows well in all light conditions from **full sun** (best fall color) to **full shade** (less arching, more upright habit). The soil should be **fertile** and **moist,** although Virginia sweetspire is fairly adaptable. Chlorosis (leaf yellowing) may occur in highly alkaline soils or during drought.

Tips

Virginia sweetspire is an excel-lent shrub for low-lying and moist areas. It grows well near streams and water features. It is also a fine choice for plantings in areas where the scent of the fragrant flowers can be enjoyed. Virginia sweet-spire can be used individually or in small groups in the home garden, and it looks awesome mass planted in large areas.

Recommended

I. virginica is an upright to arching, suckering shrub that usually grows wider than tall. Spikes of fragrant, white flowers appear in late spring. The leaves turn shades of purple and red in fall.

I. virginica (above & below)

Virginia sweetspire has been refined from its wild, straggly habit, and recent cultivars offer neat, compact additions to the shrub border.

Features: attractive habit; fragrant, white flowers; fall color **Habit:** upright to arching, deciduous shrub **Height:** 2–6' **Spread:** 3–6' or more **Hardiness:** zones: 5–9

Yellow Bells
Forsythia

F. x intermedia (above & below)

Yellow bells can be used as a hedging plant, but it looks most attractive and flowers best when grown informally.

ellow bells is great when it bursts into bloom after a long, colorless winter, but it just seems to take up garden space once it is done flowering.

Growing

Yellow bells grows best in **full sun**. The soil should be of **average fertility, moist** and **well drained**. Established shrubs are extremely drought tolerant.

Tips

Include yellow bells in a shrub or mixed border where other flowering plants will provide interest once yellow bells' early-season glory has passed. It is great as a trellis for clematis to climb through. New selections with decorative foliage are being introduced to the market each year.

Recommended

F. x *intermedia* is a large shrub with upright stems that arch as they mature. It grows 6–10' tall and 6–12' wide. Bright yellow flowers emerge in early to mid-spring, before the leaves. Many cultivars of various sizes and forms are available. A few of the better choices include GOLDEN PEEP and GOLD TIDE and the variegated selections 'Fiesta' and 'Kumson.'

Features: attractive yellow early to mid-spring flowers **Habit:** spreading, deciduous shrub with upright or arching branches **Height:** 6–10' **Spread:** 6–12' **Hardiness:** zones 5–8

Yucca

Yucca

Planted alone or en masse, yucca makes a strong architectural statement.

Growing

Yucca grows best in **full sun,** in **light, sandy, well-drained, neutral to slightly acidic** soil, but it adapts to most well-drained soils.

Pruning is not needed, but the flower spikes can be removed when flowering is finished, and dead leaves can be removed as needed.

Tips

Yucca looks great as an accent plant in beds, borders and foundation plantings. It also looks good as a specimen in pots, planters and urns. The variegated varieties add color and texture to beds and borders.

Recommended

Y. gloriosa is an erect, slow-growing shrub. It has 24–36" long, sword-like, blue-green to dark green leaves that arise from a basal rosette. With age, the plant develops a thick trunk and loses its lower leaves. Old plants may also develop branches, with a rosette of foliage atop each branch. The fragrant, purple-tinged, white flowers are held above the foliage on tall, spike-like clusters.

The leaves of Y. gloriosa have smooth margins and are not as stiff (or as hazardous) as those of close relatives Y. filamentosa (Adam's needle) and Y. aloifolia (Spanish bayonet).

Also called: Spanish dagger, mound-lily yucca
Features: white summer flowers; striking foliage; appealing habit **Habit:** rounded rosette of long, stiff, spiky, evergreen leaves
Height: 4–6'; up to 8' when flowering
Spread: 4–6' **Hardiness:** zones 6–10

Blanc Double de Coubert

Rugosa Shrub Rose

The soft petals of Blanc Double de Coubert are easily marked by rain, which may cause the flowers to appear spent not long after they open.

Every rose garden should include one of these magnificent rugosa roses. A beautiful rose, over a century old, it has a fascinating history and an outstanding reputation.

Growing

This hardy rugosa prefers **full sun** but tolerates light shade. **Organically rich**, **moist**, **well-drained** soil is best, but most soils are adequate. Blanc Double de Coubert is highly resistant to disease.

Tips

Blanc Double de Coubert is excellent for hedging and borders, or planted as a specimen. The blossoms are ideal for cutting as well—for best vase life, cut them when they are still partially closed.

Recommended

Rosa 'Blanc Double de Coubert' is a moderately vigorous, dense shrub with arching branches. It bears fragrant, loosely petalled, white, semi-double blossoms followed by hips that transform into reddish orange spheres and stand out among the stunning fall foliage.

Features: hardy; strongly scented, white flowers in early summer and fall **Height:** 4–7' **Spread:** 4–7' **Hardiness:** zones 3–8

Butterfly Rose

Old Garden (China) Rose

The butterfly rose's vermilion buds give way to buff yellow flowers that soon become shades of pink and finally deep crimson. This changing color palette is an unusual but desirable trait that will brighten the gloomiest site.

Growing

This rose prefers **full sun** and **fertile, moist, well-drained** soil with at least **5% organic matter** mixed in. Butterfly rose tolerates shade but is not fond of cold wind. A heavy feeder and drinker, it does not like to share its root space with other plants.

Tips

Butterfly rose requires very little maintenance. It works best as a specimen, but it makes a wonderful informal hedge. Its foliage contrasts well with lighter foliage on other plants. This suckering rose is also good for hillside plantings.

Recommended

Rosa chinensis var. ***mutabilis*** (*R. odorata* 'Mutabilis') has soft, red stems and glossy, red-tinged, dark green foliage. Plant size and shape vary with location. Some people claim this rose can grow 10–25' high.

Mutabilis is Latin for 'changing,' possibly a reference to the changing color of the petals on this rose.

Also called: tipo idéale, 'Mutabilis'
Features: repeat blooming; yellow mid-summer flowers that turn pink and then crimson; disease-resistant foliage **Height:** 4–6'
Spread: 3–5' **Hardiness:** zones 5–10

Cécile Brünner

Polyantha Rose

This beloved old-timer is much admired for its small, classically shaped blooms, which appear almost continuously from early summer to fall.

Growing

Cécile Brünner prefers **full sun** and **fertile, humus-rich, slightly acidic, moist, well-drained** soil.

Because it frequently adorned buttonholes in the early 1900s, Cécile Brünner was often called the 'boutonniere rose.'

Tips

Cécile Brünner works well when used in mixed beds and borders, or as part of a foundation planting. It also does great in containers.

Recommended

Rosa 'Cécile Brünner' is a small plant with upright stems and sparse, disease-resistant, dark green foliage. This long-lived variety with almost-thornless stems bears urn-shaped, light pink, fully double flowers that have a sweet, slightly spicy fragrance. It blooms from early summer to fall, prolifically at first, then sporadically. A vigorous, climbing form that grows 20' tall and wide is available.

Also called: sweetheart rose, Maltese rose, mignon **Features:** repeat to almost continuous blooming; light pink flowers **Height:** 24–36" **Spread:** 24" **Hardiness:** zones 5–9

Cherokee Rose

Species Rose

With its stunningly beautiful flowers, it is no wonder we chose Cherokee rose as our official state flower. Cherokee rose is native to China, but it has naturalized throughout the Southeast.

Growing

Cherokee rose grows best in **full sun,** in **average to fertile, humus-rich, slightly acidic, moist, well-drained** soil. It tolerates partial shade, occasional flooding and the occasional drought. It can adapt to most soils, from sandy soil to silty clay. Provide **shelter** from cold, drying winds.

Tips

Cherokee rose makes a very effective screen and an impenetrable barrier. It grows over or through anything nearby, such as other plants, trellises, fences, pergolas and so on. In the open, it forms a large, mounded, tangled mass of stems. Cherokee rose does very well next to water features.

Recommended

Rosa laevigata is a large, vigorous, spreading, relatively pest-free rose with long, arching stems and large, hooked prickles. It bears leathery, shiny, dark green foliage. The fragrant, large, white, single flowers with bright gold stamens appear from early to mid-spring. The pear-shaped hips are reddish brown and covered in stiff bristles.

Cherokee rose became Georgia's official state flower on August 18, 1916, when a joint resolution was passed by the General Assembly and approved by Governor Nathaniel Harris.

Features: attractive foliage; fragrant, white flowers; low maintenance; easy to grow
Height: 6–10' **Spread:** 10–15'
Hardiness: zones 7–9

Dortmund

Climbing Rose

*F*ew roses are rated as highly and respected as much as Dortmund. The foliage alone makes it worthwhile.

Growing

Plant in **full sun,** in **fertile, humus-rich, slightly acidic, moist, well-drained** soil. Dortmund requires reasonably good growing conditions to thrive, but it tolerates light, dappled shade and poorer soils and is highly disease resistant.

Deadhead heavily and frequently to encourage blooming. Discontinue deadheading at least five weeks before first frost to allow the plant to form a large crop of bright red hips in fall.

Tips

This rose can grow large enough to cover one side of a small building. To create a medium shrub useful for hedging or as a specimen, prune to control the size. As a climber, it can be trained up a pillar, veranda post, wall or trellis. It can also be grafted as a weeping standard.

Recommended

Rosa 'Dortmund' is a tall, upright plant with dense, glossy, dark green foliage. Dortmund blooms from spring to fall, with the majority of flowers occurring in spring. Blooming is a little slow to start, but, once it begins to take off, the results are worth the wait. The flowers have a light apple scent, and each large, red flower has a glowing central white eye and bright yellow stamens.

Features: attractive foliage and habit; abundant white-eyed, red flowers; repeat blooming
Height: 14–24' **Spread:** 8–10'
Hardiness: zones 5–9

Gourmet Popcorn

Miniature Rose

Gourmet Popcorn bears cascading clusters of honey-scented, rounded, white, semi-double flowers with short stems.

Growing

Gourmet Popcorn prefers **full sun** and **fertile, moist, well-drained** soil with at least **5% organic matter** mixed in. It can tolerate light breezes but keep it out of strong winds. Roses are heavy feeders and drinkers, and they do not like to share their root space with other plants.

Tips

Gourmet Popcorn looks stunning planted en masse or in pots, containers and hanging baskets. Plant this rose where its fragrance can be enjoyed—alongside pathways, under windows or next to a garden bench.

In warm regions, Gourmet Popcorn can grow up to twice its typical height, creating an impressive specimen with hundreds of flowers in bloom at a time.

Recommended

Rosa '**Gourmet Popcorn**' is a vigorous, compact, cushion-like, rounded shrub with lush, dark green foliage. It is highly resistant to disease and virtually maintenance free.

Also called: Summer Snow **Features:** attractive form; repeat blooming; abundant white flowers from summer to fall **Height:** 18–24"
Spread: 24" **Hardiness:** zones 4–9

Gruss an Aachen

Floribunda Rose

Gruss an Aachen was hybridized in 1909, before the floribunda class was invented. This low-maintenance, easy-to-grow rose is still popular today.

Growing

Gruss an Aachen grows well in **full sun** or **partial shade,** in **slightly acidic, moist, well-drained** soil of **average fertility.** Using an organic mulch helps keep the soil moist and the roots cool. Flowering and disease resistance are best in full sun. Deadheading helps encourage more flowers through the season.

Tips

Gruss an Aachen can be used alone or in groups in shrub or mixed beds and borders, as informal hedges and in containers.

Recommended

Rosa 'Gruss an Aachen' is a small, rounded, vigorous, bushy shrub with thin, arching stems and few prickles. The leathery, somewhat glossy and rich to dark green foliage is disease resistant. From orange-red and yellow flower buds come large, light to flesh pink, very double flowers that fade to creamy white with age and have a mild, sweet fragrance. This sterile plant does not form hips.

The name Gruss an Aachen means 'Greetings to Aachen.' Aachen is the German home town of this rose's breeder, Philipp Geduldig.

Also called: Salut d'Aix la Chapelle
Features: repeat blooming; light pink flowers, fading to creamy white, from spring to fall
Height: 18–30" **Spread:** 24–36"
Hardiness: zones (5)6–9

Iceberg
Floribunda Rose

Over 40 years have passed since this exceptional rose was first introduced into commerce, and its continued popularity proves it can stand the test of time.

Growing
Iceberg grows best in **full sun**. The soil should be **fertile, humus rich, slightly acidic, moist** and **well drained**.

Tips
Iceberg is a popular addition to mixed borders and beds, and it also works well as a specimen. Plant it in a well-used area or near a window, where the fragrance of its flowers can best be enjoyed. This rose can also be included in large planters or patio containers.

Recommended
Rosa '**Iceberg**' is a vigorous shrub with a rounded, bushy habit and light green foliage. The clusters of semi-double flowers are produced in several flushes from early to mid-summer. The white flowers are sometimes flushed with pink during cool or wet weather. A climbing variation of this rose is also available.

Iceberg blooms tend to be flushed with pink when the nights are cool. Rain or dewdrops can also cause pink stains.

Also called: Fée des Neiges **Features:** bushy habit; strong, sweet fragrance; white early to mid-summer flowers **Height:** 36"–4'
Spread: 36"–4' **Hardiness:** zones 5–8

Knockout

Modern Shrub Rose

This rose is simply one of the best new shrub roses to hit the market in years.

Growing

Knockout grows best in **full sun**. The soil should be **fertile, humus rich, slightly acidic, moist** and **well drained**. This rose blooms most prolifically in warm weather but has deeper red flowers in cooler weather. Deadhead lightly to keep the plant tidy and to encourage prolific blooming.

Tips

This vigorous rose makes a good addition to a mixed bed or border, and it is attractive when planted in groups of three or more. It can be mass planted to create a large display, or grown singly as an equally beautiful specimen.

Recommended

Rosa 'Knockout' has a lovely rounded form and glossy, green leaves that turn to shades of burgundy in fall. The bright, cherry red flowers are borne in clusters of 3–15 almost all summer and beyond, and the orange-red hips persist for much of winter. **'Double Knockout,' 'Pink Knockout'** and a light pink selection called **'Blushing Knockout'** are also available. All have excellent disease resistance.

Also called: Knock Out **Features:** rounded habit; lightly tea rose–scented, cherry red to light pink flowers from mid-summer to fall; disease resistant **Height:** 3–4'
Spread: 3–4' **Hardiness:** zones 4–10

Marchesa Boccella

Old Garden (Portland) Rose

Because there is no proof of the breeder or location and date of origin for Marchesa Boccella, some growers debate whether it and Jacques Cartier are the same rose. At rose shows, this variety is required to be called Marchesa Boccella, but it is typically known throughout North America as Jacques Cartier.

Growing

Marchesa Boccella prefers **full sun,** in **fertile, moist, well-drained** soil. Use mulch to retain moisture and keep the roots cool. Heavy pruning may be needed to stimulate lush, new growth.

Tips

Marchesa Boccella is highly disease resistant and easy to grow. It excels in containers, as hedging and in mixed beds or borders.

Recommended

Rosa **'Marchesa Boccella'** is a dense, upright shrub with strong stems and a lot of prickles. Over the growing season, the leathery, light green foliage changes to blue-green. The quartered rosette, soft pink, double flowers display a green button eye and are extremely fragrant. A tendency for the flower clusters to be slightly obscured within the foliage gives the plant a neat and tidy appearance but reduces the overall impact of the blooms.

The showy, fragrant flowes of Marchesa Boccella are popular at rose shows.

Also called: Marquise Boçella, Marquise Boccella, Jacques Cartier **Features:** repeat blooming; fragrant, large, soft pink flowers from spring to fall **Height:** 3–4' **Spread:** 24–36" **Hardiness:** zones 5–9

New Dawn

Climbing Rose

New Dawn is one of the all-time favorite climbing varieties among gardeners and rosarians. In 1910, Dr. William Van Fleet of the United States introduced a hybrid seedling named 'Dr. W. Van Fleet'; it gave rise to a repeat-blooming sport introduced in 1930 as 'The New Dawn.'

Growing

New Dawn grows well in **full sun** or **partial shade**, in **fertile, moist, well-drained** soil with at least **5% organic matter** mixed in.

Tips

Considered one of the easiest climbers to grow, this rose is suitable for pergolas, walls, fences, arches or pillars or can be pruned as a hedge or shrub. It is also a good rose for exhibition.

Recommended

Rosa **'New Dawn'** is a vigorous, disease-resistant climber with upright, arching canes that support abundant, medium to dark green, shiny foliage. Borne singly or in small clusters, the double flowers have a sweet apple fragrance and fade from a soft pink to a pinkish white.

During their 1997 Triennial Convention, members of the World Federation of Rose Societies elected New Dawn into the Hall of Fame. It was celebrated as the world's first patented plant.

Also called: Everblooming Dr. W. Van Fleet, The New Dawn **Features:** repeat blooming; pale pearl pink flowers from early summer to fall; climbing habit **Height:** 15–20' **Spread:** 10–15' **Hardiness:** zones 5–9

The Fairy
Modern Shrub Rose

The Fairy is popular with both novice and experienced gardeners. It bears large clusters of dainty, rosette-shaped, soft pink, double flowers.

Growing

The Fairy grows well in **full sun** or **partial shade;** although prone to blackspot in partial shade, it will still bloom, with slower color fading. It prefers **fertile, moist, well-drained** soil with at least **5% organic matter** mixed in. Roses can tolerate light breezes but keep them out of strong winds.

Tips

This rose can be used in containers, as a groundcover, in mixed beds and borders, as a weeping standard or left to trail over a low wall or embankment. It looks great massed or planted as low hedging. It makes a beautiful cut flower and is useful for covering a stump in the sun.

Recommended

Rosa **'The Fairy'** is a compact, mounding plant with moderately prickly canes and glossy foliage. Trouble free and highly resistant to disease, it blooms continually until fall frost.

Also called: Fairy, Feerie **Features:** repeat blooming; soft pink flowers from late summer to fall; low maintenance **Height:** 24" **Spread:** 2–4' **Hardiness:** zones 4–9

Big-leaf Periwinkle
Vinca

V. minor (above), *V. major* 'Variegata' (below)

Big-leaf periwinkle is a dependable spreading groundcover, and one plant can cover almost any size area. Its reliability is second to none, and its ease of growth is sure to please.

Growing

Big-leaf periwinkle grows best in **partial to full shade**, in **fertile, moist, well-drained** soil. It adapts to many types of soil, but it turns yellow if the soil is too dry or the sun is too hot. Divide in early spring or fall, or whenever it becomes overgrown.

Tips

Big-leaf periwinkle is a useful and attractive groundcover in a shrub border,

under trees or on a shady bank, and it prevents soil erosion. It is shallow rooted and able to outcompete weeds but won't interfere with deeper-rooted shrubs.

If big-leaf periwinkle begins to outgrow its space, it may be sheared back hard in early spring. The sheared-off ends may have rooted along the stems; these rooted cuttings may be transplanted or potted and given away as gifts.

Recommended

V. major forms a mat of vigorous, upright to trailing stems bearing evergreen, dark green foliage. Purple to violet blue flowers are borne in a flush in spring and sporadically throughout summer. **'Variegata'** has leaves with creamy white edges.

V. minor (lesser periwinkle) forms a low, loose mat of trailing stems, and has smaller flowers and foliage than *V. major*.

Also called: greater periwinkle, myrtle
Features: trailing foliage; purple to violet blue flowers **Height:** 10–18" **Spread:** 18" to indefinite **Hardiness:** zones 6–9

Carolina Jasmine

Gelsemium

Carolina jasmine is known to scamper up large trees, fences and even utility poles. Golden yellow flowers adorn this sprawling vine in late winter, reminding us that spring is just around the corner.

Growing

Carolina jasmine grows well in **full sun** (shrubby and compact) or **partial shade** (much taller, with fewer flowers). The soil should be **fertile, organically rich, moist** and **well drained**.

Pinch the new growth back to encourage a denser growth habit. When the growth is thin at the bottom, and the top is falling over because of the weight, cut this vine back to approximately 24–36" high.

Tips

Carolina jasmine can be grown on a decorative trellis, pergola or arbor. It is often used to adorn mailboxes and just about anything that requires a bit of color and a vertical element.

All parts of this plant are highly **poisonous**. Ingestion could be fatal.

Recommended

G. sempervirens is a vigorous, twining, woody vine with glossy, dark green foliage. It produces masses of fragrant, funnel-shaped, golden to pale yellow flowers in late winter to spring.

G. sempervirens (above & below)

Carolina jasmine makes an effective low-maintenance groundcover for shaded areas and on hard-to-maintain slopes.

Also called: Carolina jessamine
Features: bright to pale yellow flowers; attractive foliage; twining habit **Height:** 10–20'
Spread: 4–5' **Hardiness:** zones 6–10

Climbing Hydrangea

Hydrangea

H. anomala subsp. *petiolaris* (above & below)

A mature climbing hydrangea can cover an entire wall. With its glossy, dark green leaves and delicate, lacy flowers, climbing hydrangea is quite possibly one of the most stunning climbing plants available.

Growing

Climbing hydrangea prefers **partial or light shade** but tolerates full sun or full shade. The soil should be of **average to high fertility, humus rich, moist** and **well drained**. This plant performs best in cool, moist conditions, so put it on the north or east side of buildings, and be sure to mulch the roots. Typically slow to establish, it exhibits fast growth beginning in its third year.

Tips

Climbing hydrangea climbs up trees, walls, fences, pergolas and arbors. It clings to walls by means of aerial roots and needs no support, just a somewhat textured surface, such as concrete blocks. It also grows over rocks and can be used as a groundcover—or train it to form a small tree or shrub.

Recommended

H. anomala subsp. *petiolaris* (*H. petiolaris*) is a clinging vine with glossy, dark green leaves that sometimes turn an attractive yellow in fall. For more than a month in mid-summer, when lacy-looking, white flowers cover the vine, the entire plant appears to be veiled in a lacy mist.

Climbing hydrangea produces the most flowers when it is exposed to some direct sunlight each day.

Features: large, lacy, white flowers; clinging habit; exfoliating bark **Height:** 50–80'
Spread: up to 4' for individual plants; 50' or more as a groundcover **Hardiness:** zones 4–8

Five-leaf Akebia

Akebia

This vigorous vine twines up anything that gets in its way. It can become invasive, so keep the pruning shears handy if you plan to sit near it. It can be evergreen near the coast, especially when planted close to a house.

Growing

Five-leaf akebia grows equally well in **full sun, light shade** or **partial shade,** in **well-drained** soil of **average to high fertility**. It tolerates dry or moist soils and full shade.

Tips

Five-leaf akebia quickly covers any sturdy structure, such as a porch railing, trellis, pergola, arbor or fence. Cut the plant back as much and as often as needed to keep it under control. Prune off the fruits to diminish self-seeding.

Although this vine has fragrant flowers and interesting fruit, it is worth growing for the foliage alone.

A. quinata (above & below)

Recommended

A. *quinata* is a fast-growing, twining, deciduous climbing vine. Tinged purple in spring, the foliage matures to an attractive blue-green. Deep purple flowers borne in spring are followed by sausage-like fruit pods. **'Alba'** bears white flowers and fruit.

Bearing fragrant blooms as a bonus, five-leaf akebia can quickly provide privacy and shade when grown over a chain-link fence or on a trellis next to a porch.

Features: attractive foliage; twining habit; purple or white flowers; fruit **Height:** 20–40' **Spread:** 20–40' **Hardiness:** zones 5–8

Green and Gold

Chrysogonum

C. virginianum (above & below)

Green and gold definitely prefers our Southern climates and soils, and it is sure to impress with its bright yellow blossoms and attractive green foliage.

Growing

Green and gold prefers **partial to full shade** but tolerates full sun at the northern edge of our state; flowering is decreased in full shade. Green and gold adapts to most **moist, well-drained** soils, although adding extra **organic matter** to the soil benefits the plant.

Tips

This spreading perennial is often used as a flowering groundcover. For a blast of bright color, it can be used in woodland or native gardens and at the front of perennial or shrub borders.

Recommended

C. virginianum forms an attractive mat of toothed, coarse-textured foliage that spreads by runners that root at the nodes. Starry-shaped, bright yellow flowers bloom prolifically in early spring and in fall, with sporadic blooms throughout summer. A number of cultivars are available with dark green leaves, wider spreads, longer blooming periods or more vigorous growth habits.

Also called: golden star **Features:** bright yellow flowers; lush foliage; attractive habit **Height:** 8–10" **Spread:** 18–24" **Hardiness:** zones 5–8

Hyacinth Bean

Lablab (Dolichos)

L. purpureus (above & below)

Hyacinth beans are like sweet peas on steroids. The vines grow profusely and provide great visual interest, including the iridescent purple seedpods. When cooked carefully, the pods can double as a food crop.

Growing

Hyacinth bean prefers **full sun**. The soil should be **fertile, moist** and **well drained**.

Tips

Hyacinth bean needs a trellis, net, pole or other structure to twine up. Plant it against a fence or near a balcony. If you grow it as a groundcover, make sure it doesn't engulf smaller plants.

The raw beans contain a cyanide-releasing chemical, so never eat the beans unless they are thoroughly cooked, using two to four changes of water.

Recommended

L. purpureus (*Dolichos lablab*) is a vigorously twining vine. It can grow up to 30' tall, but it reaches only about 10–15' tall when grown as an annual. The many purple or white summer flowers are followed by attractive deep purple pods.

Using hyacinth bean plants and six to eight bamboo poles that are 6' tall, you can create a living teepee—the perfect hiding place to bring a smile to a child's face.

Also called: Egyptian bean, lablab bean, lablab, Indian bean **Features:** large, bold leaves; attractive habit; sweet pea–like flowers in purple or white **Height:** 10–15' **Spread:** variable **Hardiness:** treat as an annual

Ivy
Hedera

H. helix (above & below)

Ivy is a popular houseplant and is frequently used in wire-frame topiaries.

One of the loveliest things about ivy is the variation in green and blue tones it adds to the garden.

Growing

Ivy prefers **light or partial shade** but adapts to any light condition from full shade to full sun; on a sunny, exposed site, the foliage can become damaged or dried out in winter. The soil should be of **average to high fertility, moist** and **well drained**. The richer the soil, the better this vine grows.

Tips

Ivy is grown as a trailing groundcover that roots at the stem nodes or as a climbing vine. It clings tenaciously to house walls, tree trunks, stumps and many other rough-textured surfaces. Ivy rootlets can damage walls and fences, and ivy can be invasive in warm climates. Choose small-leaved cultivars for slower growth.

Recommended

H. helix is a vigorous plant with triangular, evergreen, glossy, dark green leaves that may be tinged with bronze or purple in winter, adding another season of interest to your garden. Many cultivars have been developed. Some cultivars have interesting, often variegated foliage. Check with your local garden center to see what is available.

Also called: common ivy, English ivy
Features: decorative foliage; climbing or trailing habit **Height:** 6–8" as a groundcover; up to 90' when climbing **Spread:** indefinite
Hardiness: zones 5–9

Lily Turf
Liriope

*L*ily turf is an excellent ground-cover plant that grows so thick that weeds can't compete. It is very easy to grow, relatively problem free, easy to obtain and tough as nails.

Growing

Lily turf prefers to grow in **partial or light shade,** in **moderately fertile, humus-rich, moist, well-drained** soil, but it can adapt to full sun or full shade and most well-drained soils. Divide in spring as new growth resumes.

Tips

Lily turf can be used as a dense groundcover and for erosion control. It looks great when planted in mass drifts and reduces the amount of mulch needed each year. Lily turf grows well under large deciduous trees, and it does well in containers. To encourage new growth, trim or remove winter-damaged foliage in late winter or early spring.

Recomended

L. muscari is a slow-spreading, clump-forming, evergreen perennial that has wide, arching, grass-like, dark green foliage. The spikes of late-summer flowers, in violet purple to white, are held above the foliage. Persistent, shiny, black or white berries follow. **'Variegata'** has lavender purple flowers; its foliage has creamy yellow edges.

L. muscari (above), *L. muscari* 'Variegata' (below)

Not a true grass, lily turf is actually a member of the lily family.

Also called: blue lily turf, border grass
Features: strap-like foliage; easy to grow; purple to white flowers **Height:** 12–18"
Spread: 6–12" **Hardiness:** zones 6–10

Mondo Grass

Ophiopogon

O. japonicus cultivar (above & below)

asy to grow and dependable, mondo grass is dense enough to outcompete weeds and requires very minimal maintenance. It is a great groundcover for shady places where not much else will grow.

Growing

Mondo grass prefers **partial to full, dense shade** and **moist, moderately fertile, well-drained, humus-rich** soil. Divide in spring, just as new growth appears. Apply some good compost or leaf mold around the plants in fall. In the far north of Georgia, this plant appreciates the **protection** of some thick mulch for winter.

Tips

Mondo grass is best used as a dense groundcover and for erosion control. It is also useful for edging beds and borders, and it does quite well in containers. The smaller cultivars are great in rock gardens and between stepping stones.

Recomended

O. japonicus is a clump-forming, evergreen perennial that spreads quickly by rhizomes. It has narrow, arching, grass-like, dark green foliage. Short clusters of white flowers, possibly with purple tinges, nestle in the foliage in summer; they are followed by persistent, shiny, black-blue berries. **'Compactus'** ('Nana') forms a dense mat of dark green foliage 2" tall. **'Kyoto Dwarf'** grows 4" tall and wide. **'Silver Mist'** bears variegated, green-and-white foliage.

Also called: lilyturf **Features:** grass-like foliage; white or purple-tinged white flowers
Height: 2–12" **Spread:** 4–12"
Hardiness: zones 7–10

Moonflower

Ipomoea

Moonflower will embellish a chain-link fence, a wire topiary structure or any object thin enough for it to twine its tendrils around. Once it is established, stand back—this vine grows fast.

Growing

Grow moonflower in **full sun** or **partial shade,** in **light, well-drained** soil of **poor fertility**. It tolerates any type of soil. Nick the seed coat with a file and soak the seed for 24 hours before sowing. Start the seed in individual peat pots if sowing indoors. Plant in late spring.

Tips

Moonflower can be grown anywhere—on fences, walls, trees, trellises or arbors. As a groundcover, it will cover any obstacle it encounters.

This vine must twine around objects, such as wire or twine, in order to climb; wide fence posts, walls or other broad objects are too large. Secure sturdy netting to a wall to make a good climbing surface for moonflower.

Recommended

I. alba (moonflower) is a vigorous, climbing vine that has dense, dark green foliage and sweetly scented, large, trumpet-shaped, white flowers that arise from showy, spiraled flower buds. From mid-summer through fall, the flowers open in early evening.

I. alba (above & below)

Each moonflower flower lasts for only one day. The flower bud forms a spiral that slowly unfurls as the day comes to an end with the setting sun.

Features: fast growth; white flowers
Height: 10–12' **Spread:** 12–24"
Hardiness: tender perennial grown as an annual

Scarlet Trumpet Honeysuckle

Lonicera

L. *sempervirens* (above)
L. x *brownii* 'Dropmore Scarlet' (below)

Scarlet trumpet honeysuckle is a great plant for attracting hummingbirds to your garden.

Honeysuckles can be rampant growers, but with careful consideration and placement these twining vines won't overrun your garden.

Growing

Honeysuckles grow well in **full sun** or **partial shade**. The soil should be **average to fertile, humus rich, moist** and **well drained**.

Tips

Honeysuckles can be trained to grow up a trellis, fence, arbor or other structure. If grown in a large container near a porch, they will ramble over the edges of the pot and up the railings with reckless abandon.

Recommended

L. sempervirens is a moderately vigorous, deciduous, twining vine that has attractive blue-green foliage and bears orange or red flowers in mid-spring and early summer. The fruit is a round, red berry that ripens in fall. Many cultivars and hybrids have flowers in yellow, red or scarlet.

L. x *brownii* **'Dropmore Scarlet,'** one of the hardiest of the climbing honeysuckles, bears bright red flowers for most of summer. **'Sulphurea'** has yellow flowers and bright green foliage.

Dozens of other honeysuckle species, hybrids and cultivars exist, many with fragrant flowers. Check with your local garden center to see what is available.

Also called: trumpet honeysuckle, coral honeysuckle **Features:** orange, red or yellow flowers; twining habit; colorful fruit **Height:** 10–20'
Spread: 10–20' **Hardiness:** zones 4–9

Smilax

Smilax

S. lanceolata (above)

Smilax is a native vine that grows well at the edges of woodlands and swamps. The stems arise from a huge rhizome or tuber, which can weigh up to 300 pounds! High in starch, this edible rhizome was eaten by the natives of Georgia.

Growing

Smilax grows well in **full sun** or **partial shade,** in **moderate to fertile, moist** soil.

Tips

Smilax climbs by use of tendrils, so it needs a structure or surface that the tendrils can wrap around.

Smilax makes an excellent screen on a tall fence or trellis. Male and female flowers are borne on separate plants, and both male and female plants are needed for fruit to form.

Because of its thorns, it is best to avoid *S. rotundifolia.*

Recommended

S. lanceolata is a vigorous, twining, thicket-forming, evergreen vine with lance-shaped, shiny, medium to dark green foliage with blotchy, lighter green undersides. It bears jasmine-scented, green flowers in mid-spring and early summer. The small, rounded fruit is black when mature. The stems are not as prickly as with other *Smilax* species; the majority of prickles, if any, are at the stem nodes.

Also called: lanceleaf greenbrier, bamboo brier, Virginia sarsaparilla **Features:** fast growth; attractive foliage **Height:** 20–40 ' **Spread:** 2–5' **Hardiness:** zones 7–10

Many animals use smilax for food. Deer, cattle and sheep browse on the stems and leaves, and many species of birds enjoy the fruit.

Sweet Autumn Clematis

Clematis

C. paniculata (above & below)

Sweet autumn clematis is an attractive, tough, low-maintenance, easy-to-grow vine that can take over the garden if you are not paying attention.

Many types of clematis are available in different forms and sizes, bearing a wide array of colored flowers in many varied styles and with different bloom times.

Growing

Sweet autumn clematis prefers **full sun** but tolerates partial shade. The soil should be **fertile, humus rich, moist** and **well drained**. This vine enjoys some **shelter** from winter winds and warm, sunny weather, but the roots prefer to be cool. The rootball should be planted about 2" beneath the surface of the soil. A thick layer of mulch or a planting of low, shade-providing perennials helps protect the tender roots.

Tips

Sweet autumn clematis can climb up structures, such as trellises, railings, fences or arbors with a sturdy constitution. It can also be allowed to grow over shrubs or up trees, or grown as groundcover.

Recommended

C. paniculata (*C. maximowicziana, C. terniflora*), one of the best *Clematis* species for our hot climate, is a vigorous, twining vine. A deciduous or semi-evergreen climber, it has lush, deep green foliage. The fragrant, star-shaped, white flowers of late summer and early fall are followed by decorative seedheads. Where it is happy, this vine self-seeds with too much gusto and should be cut back before that can occur.

Features: twining habit; fast growth; white flowers; decorative seedheads **Height:** 15–20' **Spread:** 6–10' **Hardiness:** zones 4–8

Trumpet Creeper
Campsis

C. radicans (above), *C. radicans* cultivar (below)

rumpet creeper is a chugging loco-motive of a plant that can cover just about any structure in less than five years.

Growing

This heat-tolerant vine flowers best in **full sun** but also grows well in partial or light shade. Growth is most rampant in **fertile** soil, but almost any soil will do.

Tips

Trumpet creeper clings to any surface—a wall, a tree, a fence or a telephone pole—but the aerial rootlets can damage painted surfaces. One plant can provide a privacy screen very quickly, or it can be grown up an exterior wall or over the porch of a house. Trumpet creeper can be used on arbors and trellises, but it needs frequent pruning to stay attractive and within bounds. Once you have one of these vines, you will probably never get rid of it.

Also called: trumpet vine, hummingbird vine
Features: clinging habit; orange, red or yellow flowers; easy to grow **Height:** 30–40'
Spread: 30–40' **Hardiness:** zones 4–9

Recommended

C. radicans is a fast-growing, deciduous vine that climbs by aerial rootlets. It spreads by suckers and can form large, thick colonies. For a long period in summer, it bears trumpet-shaped, dark orange flowers. **'Crimson Trumpet'** has bright red flowers. **'Flava'** bears yellow flowers.

Hummingbirds are attracted to trumpet creeper's long, tube-like flowers.

Trumpet Flower

Bignonia

B. capreolata 'Jeckyll' (above & below)

Trumpet flower is sometimes confused with trumpet creeper. Although they look somewhat similar, trumpet flower blooms earlier in the season and doesn't have the same invasive nature.

This native vine is known to grow very large and at a rapid rate. It blooms like crazy and will disguise unsightly surfaces and structures in no time.

Growing

Trumpet flower prefers **full sun** and **organically rich, well-drained** soil, but it can tolerate a wide range of soil conditions. Partial shade results in reduced flowering. When the plant outgrows its allotted space, prune it after flowering.

Tips

This twining plant climbs up just about anything. The stems climb by tendrils and by holdfast disks (little suction cup–like bits) at the ends of their tendrils. After planting a trumpet flower, attach it to the surface or structure it will eventually climb. Any type of garden structure will work, along with stone or brick walls, fences, poles and trees.

Recommended

B. capreolata is a vigorous, twining vine that produces lush, semi-evergreen to evergreen, dark green foliage. The foliage takes on a purplish red color in cold weather. Moderately fragrant, the tubular, orange-yellow flowers with reddish throats emerge in spring and early summer. Cultivars are available in many fiery colors.

Also called: cross vine **Features:** bright, fiery colored flowers; vigorous, twining habit
Height: 30–50' **Spread:** 20–40'
Hardiness: zones 6–9

Virginia Creeper
Parthenocissus

Let a Virginia creeper adorn any garden that needs a look of wild abandon. Every fall, Virginia creeper explodes in a wildfire of color.

Growing
These vines grow well in any light from **full sun to full shade**. The soil should be **fertile** and **well drained**. The plants adapt to clay or sandy soils.

Tips
Virginia creeper and Boston ivy do not require support, because they have clinging rootlets that can adhere to just about any surface, even smooth wood, vinyl or metal. Give the plants a lot of space and let them cover a wall, fence or arbor. They can also be used as groundcovers.

Recommended
Virginia creeper and Boston ivy are very similar, except for the shape of the leaves. The fruits of both are **poisonous**.

P. quinquefolia (Virginia creeper, woodbine) has dark green foliage. Each leaf, divided into five leaflets, turns flame red in fall.

P. tricuspidata (Boston ivy, Japanese creeper) has dark green, three-lobed leaves that turn red in fall. This species is not quite as hardy or as fast growing as Virginia creeper.

P. quinquefolia (above & below)

Virginia creeper can cover the sides of buildings and help keep them cool in the summer heat. Cut the plants back to keep windows and doors accessible.

Features: attractive foliage; fall color; clinging habit **Height:** 30–70' **Spread:** 30–70'
Hardiness: zones 3–8

Winter Jasmine

Jasminum

J. nudiflorum (above & below)

Growing

Winter jasmines grow well in **full sun** or **partial shade,** in **moderate to fertile, well-drained** soil. These drought-tolerant plants adapt to most soil conditions.

When using winter jasmines in formal settings, prune out one-third of the oldest growth each year after flowering finishes.

Tips

The long, trailing stems of winter jasmine make an excellent groundcover. Rooting where the stems touch the ground, this tough plant forms large, dense colonies. It is very effective on hard-to-access slopes and in areas with less than ideal soils. Winter jasmine can also be grown in a shrub or mixed border; when it is planted in a container, the stems can dangle over the sides.

Winter jasmine is a great plant for winter interest. The green stems stand out against our gray winter background, and the bright yellow flowers bloom very early in the growing season.

Trained as a vine to grow on a trellis, winter jasmine can reach 15' or more in height.

Recommended

J. **nudiflorum** is a spreading, mounding, deciduous plant with slender, arching to trailing, green stems. It grows 3–10' tall and spreads 4–10' wide. In winter and early spring, unscented, yellow flowers appear before the attractive shiny, dark green foliage emerges. The foliage develops no fall color.

Features: dark green foliage; yellow flowers; attractive habit **Height:** 3–10' **Spread:** 4–10'
Hardiness: zones 6–9

Wisteria

Wisteria

*L*oose clusters of purple hang like lace from the branches of a wisteria. With careful pruning, a gardener can create beautiful tree forms and attractive arbor specimens.

Growing

Wisterias grow well in **full sun** or **partial shade**. The soil should be of **average fertility, moist** and **well drained**. Too fertile a soil produces a lot of vegetative growth but very few flowers. Avoid planting wisterias near a lawn where fertilizer may leach over to your vine.

Tips

These vines require something to twine around, such as an arbor or other sturdy structure. Select a permanent site, because wisterias don't like to be moved. They may send up suckers, and branches that touch the ground can root.

All parts of wisterias are **poisonous**.

Recommended

W. floribunda (Japanese wisteria) bears fragrant, long, pendulous clusters of blue, purple, pink or white flowers in late spring, before the leaves emerge. Long, bean-like pods follow.

W. sinensis (Chinese wisteria) bears long, pendent clusters of fragrant, blue-purple flowers in late spring. **'Alba'** has white flowers.

W. sinensis (above & below)

To keep wisteria blooming sporadically all summer and until frost, prune off the flowering spikes as soon as the flowers fade. A long-handled pole pruner works well.

Features: blue, purple, pink or white flowers; decorative foliage; twining habit
Height: 20–50' or more **Spread:** 20–50' or more **Hardiness:** zones 4–8

Wood Vamp
Decumaria

D. barbara (above & below)

Tough, yet easy to control, wood vamp is a fast-growing vine for shade to partial shade.

An attractive, pest-free vine, wood vamp is great for growing up through trees. The tree's branches provide a structure to climb, and its foliage provides shade.

Growing

Wood vamp grows best in **partial shade,** in **acidic, humus-rich, moist, well-drained** soil of **average fertility,** but it adapts to full sun and to most soils that remain moist. **Shelter** from the hot sun and from strong or drying winds is appreciated.

Tips

Wood vamp works as a groundcover and as a climbing vine. It will slowly cover walls and arbors—and truly anything nearby. It clings to structures by use of aerial roots, and it tends to stay flat when grown on flat surfaces such as walls.

Recommended

D. barbara is a climbing vine with large, deciduous, shiny, dark green leaves. The fragrant, small, white flowers are borne in clusters in summer, but only on climbing plants. The gray-brown stems form an abundance of aerial roots, which the plant uses to attach itself to surfaces when it climbs. If left on its own with no structure to climb, it forms a sprawling mound of tangled stems.

Also called: climbing hydrangea
Features: attractive foliage; white summer flowers; climbing habit **Height:** 4–6' as a shrub; 10–20' or more when climbing
Spread: 6–10' **Hardiness:** zones 5–9

Blue Grape Hyacinth

Muscari

Blue grape hyacinths are among the flowers that signal the emergence of spring. The perfect accompaniment to other spring bulbs, they contrast beautifully with just about any color combination.

Growing

Blue grape hyacinths prefer **full sun** or **partial shade**. The soil should be **moist, well drained** and **organically rich**. Plant the bulbs 4" deep in fall.

Tips

Blue grape hyacinths are great for naturalizing under shrubs and trees, and they look best when planted in groups. They can be used in the rock garden and for edging beds or borders. Blue grape hyacinths look beautiful planted with perennials that will slowly envelop the tired-looking grape hyacinth foliage as they grow to full size.

Recommended

M. botryoides is a compact form that produces grass-like foliage and clusters of urn-shaped, blue flowers atop 12" tall, slender green stalks. The flowers emit a strong, musky scent. It is less invasive than other species and naturalizes in a more respectable manner.

Also called: common grape hyacinth
Features: grape-like clusters of fragrant, purple to blue flowers; attractive habit Height: 6–8"
Spread: 6–8" Hardiness: zones 3–8

Crested Iris

Iris

I. cristata (above & below)

Native to Georgia, the crested iris excels in our growing conditions. It is a neat, compact, spreading plant with attractive flowers.

Growing

Crested iris grows best in **partial shade** or **dappled light shade,** but it tolerates full sun in soil that remains moist. The soil should be of **average fertility, moist** and **well drained**.

Divide crested iris after flowering or in fall. Deadhead to keep it tidy.

Tips

All irises are popular plants for beds, borders and foundation plantings. Crested iris looks attractive in rock gardens and is magnificent for naturalizing in a woodland garden. It is a short plant, so keep it at the front of the border.

Irises can cause severe internal irritation if ingested. Always wash your hands after handling them. Avoid planting irises where children play.

Recommended

I. cristata is a compact plant with strap-like, bright green foliage and pale purple-blue flowers. Each lower petal, known as a fall, has a white patch with yellow to orange marks. This iris spreads rapidly through creeping rhizomes, forming dense colonies. Many cultivars are available.

Also called: dwarf crested iris
Features: spring flowers in many shades of purple-blue; attractive foliage **Height:** 4–8"
Spread: 6–12" **Hardiness:** zones 5–8

Daffodil

Narcissus

Many gardeners automatically think of the large, trumpet-shaped, yellow flowers when they think of daffodils, but the many varieties show considerable variation in color, form and size.

Growing

Daffodils grow best in **full sun** or **light, dappled shade**. The soil should be **average to fertile, moist** and **well drained**. Plant the bulbs when the weather cools in fall. As a guideline, measure the bulb from top to bottom and multiply that number by three to know how deeply to plant it.

Tips

Plant daffodils where they can be left to naturalize—in the light shade beneath a tree or in a woodland garden. In mixed beds and borders, the faded leaves can be hidden by the summer foliage of other plants. Large-leaved perennials such as hostas or large holly ferns make fine companion plants.

Recommended

Many species, hybrids and cultivars of daffodils are available. Flowers may be borne solitary or in clusters. Cultivars and hybrids are available in 12 different flower form categories. Choose dwarf varieties for small gardens.

Features: white, yellow, peach, orange, pink or bicolored spring flowers **Height:** 4–24" **Spread:** 4–12" **Hardiness:** zones 3–8

Drumstick Allium

Allium

A. sphaerocephalum

Drumstick alliums, with their striking, colorful, ball-like clusters of flowers, are sure to attract attention.

Growing

Drumstick alliums grow best in **full sun**. The soil should be **average to fertile, moist** and **well drained**. Plant the bulbs in fall.

Tips

Drumstick alliums are best in groups in a bed or border where they can be left to naturalize. They can self-seed when left to their own devices. The foliage, which tends to fade just as the plants come into flower, can be hidden with groundcover or a low, bushy companion plant. These plants are resistant to rabbits, squirrels and deer.

Although the leaves of drumstick alliums have an onion scent when bruised, the flowers have a sweeter fragrance.

After drumstick alliums bloom, leave their flowerheads to dry on the stems. The dry flowers provide a starry feature all summer long.

Recommended

A. sphaerocephalum is a long-lived perennial with smooth, rounded basal foliage and round clusters of brightly colored flowers on sturdy stalks.

Several other flowering onion species, hybrids and cultivars have gained popularity for their decorative flowers. *A. caeruleum* (blue globe onion) bears globe-like clusters of blue flowers. *A. giganteum* (giant onion) is a towering plant with large, globe-shaped clusters of pinky purple flowers.

Features: fuchsia pink to purple or blue summer flowers; cylindrical or strap-shaped leaves
Height: 20–36" **Spread:** 3–6"
Hardiness: zones 4–10

Fritillary

Fritillaria

F. imperalis (above & below)

With their unusual, royal-looking blossoms in early summer, fritillaries offer a formal element to an otherwise casual setting.

Growing

Fritillaries prefer **full sun** or **light shade**, in an area with **shelter** from the wind. The soil should be **coarse, organically rich, moist** and **very well drained**. It is important that the soil not be allowed to dry out. Because fritillaries do not like acidic soil, use lime when planting.

To protect the bulbs from late-spring frosts, plant them up to 9" deep in the ground, and at least 4" apart from one another. These plants can be propagated by division, offsets or seed.

Tips

Clumps of fritillaries are quite stunning among groupings of naturalized ornamental grasses or in large groupings at the back of mixed borders, where the skunk-like scent may be a little less evident. Fritillaries do well when grown among shrubbery; they won't be disturbed, and they benefit from fallen leaf matter, both as a mulch and as a source of organic matter.

Recommended

F. imperialis (crown imperial fritillary) produces a lush cluster of blade-like leaves at the base of a tall, slender flower stalk. A large grouping of pendent, bell-shaped blossoms surrounds this stalk just below its tip, which features a further cluster of green foliage. Many cultivars are available in fiery shades of orange, yellow and red.

Features: striking, pendent, orange, yellow or red flowers in early and mid-summer; attractive form **Height:** 36" **Spread:** 6–12" **Hardiness:** zones 4–8

Lily
Lilium

Asiatic hybrids (above), 'Stargazer' (below)

depending on the hybrid. If you plant a variety of cultivars, you can have lilies blooming all season.

Growing
Lilies grow best in **full sun** but like to have their **roots shaded**. The soil should be **rich in organic matter, fertile, moist** and **well drained**.

Tips
Lilies are often grouped in beds and borders and can be naturalized in woodland gardens and near water features. They look great in the back of the bed or in the center of a flower display. Grow at least three of these tall but narrow plants together to create some volume.

Recommended
The many species, hybrids and cultivars available are grouped by type. Check with your local garden center for what's available locally. **Asiatic hybrids** bear clusters of flowers in early or mid-summer and are available in a wide range of colors. **Oriental hybrids** bear fragrant clusters of large flowers in mid- or late summer, usually in white, pink or red.

A siatic lilies produce decorative clusters of large, richly colored blooms at different times of the season,

Also called: Oriental lily **Features:** early, mid- or late-season flowers in shades of orange, yellow, peach, pink, purple, red and white **Height:** 2–5' **Spread:** 12" **Hardiness:** zones 4–8

Spider Lily

Lycoris

Spider lilies are long-lived, tough, colorful plants that can handle a range of environmental conditions, from droughts to floods.

Growing

Spider lilies grow best in **full sun** or **partial shade,** in **well-drained** soil of **average fertility**. Keep them moist when in growth and allow the soil to dry during dormancy. Established plants tolerate drought. Spider lilies can be divided after they go dormant in summer. Plant the bulbs in fall, with the bulb neck at the soil surface.

Tips

Spider lilies provide color when most other plants have faded for the season. Use them in mixed beds and borders, in meadow and woodland gardens and for naturalizing.

Recommended

L. radiata is a herbaceous perennial that arises from a true bulb. Bright red flowers are borne in early fall, seemingly out of nowhere, and wither before the foliage appears. Their spidery expression is created by the long anthers (male sexual parts). The long, naked flower stalks inspired the alternative common name of naked ladies. Persisting over winter, the fleshy, strap-like basal foliage disappears by early summer.

L. radiata (above & below)

Spider lilies make great cut flowers, lasting for several days in arrangements and bouquets.

Also called: red spider lily, hurricane lily, red surprise lily, naked ladies **Features:** bright red fall flowers **Height:** 18–36" **Spread:** 6–12" **Hardiness:** zones 6–10

Star-of-Bethlehem

Ornithogalum

O. umbellatum (above & below)

Star-of-Bethlehem is a perky, attractive plant that has escaped cultivation and is now considered a weed in many states.

Many bulb plants are great for early spring color after a dull, gray Georgia winter, and star-of-Bethlehem is no exception.

Growing

Star-of-Bethlehem grows best in **full sun** or **partial shade,** in **moderately fertile, well drained** soil. It needs moisture during the growing season but can otherwise handle drought. It spreads by bulblets and seeds.

Tips

Star-of-Bethlehem is used at the front of beds and borders, in rock gardens and for naturalizing in woodland gardens. The foliage dies back after flowering, so it is best grown with plants that will cover the withering foliage as the season progresses.

All parts of the plant are **toxic,** especially the bulbs. Handling the plant may cause skin irritation. Grazing animals may be poisoned. Keep the plant away from pets and children.

Recommended

O. umbellatum is a hardy perennial bulb that forms a clump of narrow, shiny, dark green leaves 4–12" long, with a white to light green midrib. The leaves look like grass or wild garlic, but they do not have an onion or garlic aroma. The small, star-shaped, white flowers have six petals and are produced in clusters on erect stalks. The undersides of the petals have green veins.

Also called: snowdrop, nap-at-noon, sleepy-dick **Features:** easy to grow; attractive white flowers **Height:** 6–12" **Spread:** 3–6" **Hardiness:** zones 4–8

Tommies

Crocus

Tommies are harbingers of spring. The bright, cheerful colors will melt away your winter blahs. They are hardy, produce abundant flowers and are long-lived in Georgia gardens.

Growing

Tommies grow well in **full sun** or **light, dappled shade**. The soil should be **moist** and **well drained,** but not overly moist. Plant the corms 3–4" deep in fall. Where they are happy, tommies self-seed in abundance, and they can multiply quickly below ground.

Tips

Tommies and other crocuses look best when planted in groups. Drifts of tommies planted in lawns provide early color while the grass remains dormant. In beds, borders and woodland gardens, they can be left to naturalize. They fill in and spread out to provide a bright welcome in spring. Tommies are the most squirrel-resistant *Crocus* species.

Try planting tommies under decid-uous trees and shrubs. They look great under the skirt of a weeping Japanese maple or as accents for a forsythia.

Recommended

C. tommasinianus is one of the first *Crocus* species to bloom. It produces abundant silvery, pale lilac purple to dark purple to white flowers in late winter to early spring, followed by green, grass-like foliage. Many floriferous cultivars are available.

C. tommasinianus (above & below)

Saffron is obtained from the dried, crushed stigmas of C. sativus. *It takes six plants to produce enough spice for one recipe.*

Features: purple or white early-spring flowers
Height: 2–4" **Spread:** 2–4"
Hardiness: zones 4–9

Yellow Flag

Iris

I. pseudacorus (left & right)

Division is rarely required but can be done between mid-summer and fall (after flowering) to propagate new plants or when the plants begin to produce fewer flowers. Deadhead yellow flag to keep it tidy.

Irises can cause severe internal irritation if ingested. Always wash your hands after handling them. Avoid planting irises where children play.

Tips

Yellow flag is a popular border plant, alone or in groups. It is also great for the margins of a water feature and can be grown in bog gardens and in moist areas around a pond.

Recommended

I. pseudacorus is a vigorous perennial that grows 3–5' tall and forms clumps of narrow, upright leaves. In late spring and early summer, it bears bright yellow flowers with brown or purple markings. Cultivars with variegated leaves or double flowers are available.

*I*t can be difficult to find plants for wet and boggy situations, such as the areas around ponds and water features. Yellow flag loves 'wet feet' and thrives in these habitats.

Growing

Yellow flag grows well in **full sun** or **partial shade**. The soil should be of **average fertility, humus rich** and **moist to wet**. Yellow flag can grow in water up to 4" deep. Although it performs best if the soil remains consistently moist, especially in full sun, this iris does reasonably well in drier soil.

Plant yellow flag in a new pond or bog to instantly 'age' your efforts.

Features: yellow late-spring and summer flowers with brown or purple markings; attractive foliage **Height:** 3–5' **Spread:** 24" or more **Hardiness:** zones 3–8

Beebalm

Monarda

The fragrant flowers of beebalm are intoxicating to butterflies and bees—and to every passerby.

Growing

Beebalm grows well in **full sun, partial shade** or **light shade**, in **humus-rich, moist, well-drained** soil of **average fertility**. Dry conditions encourage mildew and loss of leaves. Divide every two or three years in spring, just as new growth emerges.

To extend blooming and encourage compact growth, cut back some of the stems by half in June. Thinning the stems in spring also helps prevent powdery mildew. If mildew strikes after flowering, cut the plants back to 6" to increase air circulation.

Tips

Use beebalm beside a stream or pond, or in a lightly shaded, well-watered border. It spreads in moist, fertile soils, but, as with most other members of the mint family, the shallow roots can be removed easily.

Beebalm attracts bees, butterflies and hummingbirds. Avoid using pesticides, which can seriously harm or kill these creatures and make the plant unusable for culinary or medicinal purposes.

Recommended

M. didyma is a bushy, mounding plant that forms a thick clump of stems with red or pink flowers. The many cultivars offer varied colors, sizes and levels of mildew resistance. **'Jacob Cline'** produces deep red flowers and is resistant to powdery mildew.

M. didyma 'Petite Delight' (above), *M. didyma* (below)

The fresh or dried leaves of beebalm are used to make a refreshing, minty, citrus-scented tea.

Also called: bergamot, Oswego tea
Features: fragrant, red, pink or purple flowers
Height: 2–4' **Spread:** 18–36"
Hardiness: zones 3–8

Chives

Allium

A. schoenoprasum (above & below)

Chives spread with reckless abandon as the clumps grow larger and the plants self-seed.

The delicate onion flavor of chives is best enjoyed fresh. Mix chives into dips or sprinkle them on salads and baked potatoes. Chives are said to increase appetite and encourage good digestion.

Growing

Chives grow best in **full sun**. The soil should be **fertile, moist** and **well drained,** but chives adapt to most soil conditions. These plants are easy to start from seed, but the soil temperature must be consistently above 66° F for the seeds to germinate, so seeds sown directly in the garden are unlikely to sprout before late spring or early summer. Divide in spring every few years to maintain vigor.

Tips

Chives are decorative enough to be included in a mixed or herbaceous border and can be left to naturalize. In a herb garden, chives should be given plenty of space to allow self-seeding. The edible flowers can be used in salads and for garnish. Deadheading prevents self-seeding.

Recommended

A. schoenoprasum forms a clump of cylindrical, bright green leaves. Clusters of pinky purple flowers are produced in early and mid-summer. Varieties with white or pink flowers are available.

Features: decorative foliage and habit; pink, purple or white flowers **Height:** 8–24"
Spread: 12" or more **Hardiness:** zones 3–8

Dill
Anethum

Dill leaves and seeds are probably best known for their use as pickling herbs, although they have a wide variety of other culinary uses.

Growing

Dill grows best in **full sun,** in a **sheltered** location out of strong winds. The soil should be of **poor to average fertility, moist** and **well drained**. Sow dill seeds every few weeks in spring and early summer to ensure a regular supply of leaves. Dill should not be grown near fennel, because they can cross-pollinate, causing the seeds of both plants to lose their distinct flavors.

Tips

With its feathery leaves, dill is an attractive addition to a mixed bed or border. It can be included in a vegetable garden but does well in any sunny location. Dill also attracts predatory insects and butterfly caterpillars to the garden.

Recommended

A. graveolens forms a clump of feathery foliage. Clusters of yellow flowers are borne at the tops of sturdy stems in summer. Hot or dry conditions encourage early flowering. In southern Georgia, this plant grows best in spring and fall; in the north, it grows well all summer.

A. graveolens (above & below)

Dill turns up frequently in historical records as both a culinary and medicinal herb. It was used by the ancient Egyptians and Romans and is mentioned in the Bible.

Features: edible, feathery foliage; yellow summer flowers; edible seeds **Height:** 2–5'
Spread: 12" or more **Hardiness:** annual

Fennel
Foeniculum

F. vulgare (above), F. vulgare 'Purpureum' (below)

All parts of fennel are edible, with a distinctive licorice-like fragrance and flavor. The seeds are commonly used to make a tea that is good for settling the stomach after a large meal.

Growing

Fennel grows best in **full sun**. The soil should be **average to fertile, moist** and **well drained**. Avoid planting near dill and coriander, because cross-pollination reduces seed production and makes the seed flavor of each less distinct.

Tips

Fennel is an attractive addition to a mixed bed or border. It does well in any sunny location and can be included in a vegetable garden. Fennel is good for attracting pollinators and predatory insects to the garden. To collect the seeds, remove the seed-bearing stems before the seeds start to fall off. Ensure the seeds are thoroughly dry before storing.

Recommended

F. vulgare is a short-lived perennial that forms clumps of loose, feathery, bright green foliage. Clusters of small, yellow flowers are borne in late summer. The seeds ripen in late summer or fall. A large, edible bulb-like structure forms at the stem base of the biennial **var. azoricum** (Florence fennel). This 'bulb' is popular raw in salads, cooked in soups or stews and roasted with root vegetables. **'Purpureum'** resembles the species but has bronzy purple foliage.

Features: fragrant, attractive foliage; yellow flowers; edible seeds and stems **Height:** 2–6' **Spread:** 12–24" **Hardiness:** zones 4–9

Mint

Mentha

The cool, refreshing flavor of mint lends itself to tea and other hot or cold beverages. Mint sauce, made from freshly chopped leaves, is often served with lamb.

Growing

Mints grow well in **full sun** or **partial shade**. The soil should be **average to fertile, humus rich** and **moist**. These plants spread vigorously by rhizomes and may need a barrier in the soil to restrict their spread.

Tips

Mint is a good groundcover for damp spots. Try planting it under a hose bib, where the dripping water will encourage thick growth that blocks out weeds. It grows well along ditches that may only be periodically wet. It can also be used in beds and borders, but it may overwhelm less vigorous plants.

The flowers attract bees, butterflies and other pollinators to the garden.

Recommended

Many species, hybrids and cultivars of mint are available. *M.* x *piperita* (peppermint), *M.* x *piperita citrata* (orange mint) and *M. spicata* (spearmint) are three of the most commonly grown culinary varieties. More decorative varieties with variegated leaves, such as *M.* x *gracilis* 'Variegata' (variegated ginger mint), or curly leaves as well as varieties with fruit-scented leaves are also available.

M. x *piperata* (above)
M. x *gracilis* 'Variegata' (decorative cultivar; below)

A few sprigs of fresh mint added to a pitcher of iced tea gives it an extra zip. Alternatively, pour boiling water over several types of fresh-picked mint, steep for two minutes, then enjoy hot or cold.

Features: fragrant foliage; purple, pink or white summer flowers **Height:** 6–36"
Spread: 36" or more **Hardiness:** zones 4–8

Oregano
Origanum

Oregano is one of the best known and most frequently used herbs. It is popular in stuffings, soups and stews, and no pizza is complete until it has been sprinkled with fresh or dried oregano leaves.

Growing

Most oregano grows best in **full sun,** although cultivars and varieties with golden foliage prefer partial shade, especially from the hot afternoon sun. The soil should be of **poor to average fertility, neutral to alkaline** and **well drained**. The flowers attract pollinators to the garden.

Tips

This bushy perennial makes a lovely addition to any border and can be trimmed to form low hedges. Low-growing varieties do well in the rock garden and look especially attractive combined with variegated and golden sage.

O. vulgare 'Polyphant' (above)
O. vulgare 'Aureum' (below)

In Greek, oros means 'mountain' and ganos means 'joy,' so oregano translates as 'joy of the mountain.'

Recommended

O. vulgare var. **hirtum** (oregano, Greek oregano) is the most flavorful culinary variety of oregano. This mounding perennial has hairy, gray-green leaves and white summer flowers. Many interesting varieties are available, including ones with golden, variegated or curly leaves.

Features: fragrant foliage; white flowers; bushy habit **Height:** 12–24" **Spread:** 12–24"
Hardiness: zones 4–8

Parsley
Petroselinum

Often used simply as a garnish, parsley is rich in vitamins and minerals and is reputed to freshen the breath after garlic or onion-rich foods are eaten.

Growing
Parsley grows well in **full sun** or **partial shade**. The soil should be of **average to high fertility, humus rich, moist** and **well drained**. Plants may suffer in the summer heat, but they recover as the weather cools in fall.

Parsley resents transplanting. Direct sow the seeds into warm soil or keep the soil warm with a frost sleeve, cloche, row cover or portable cold frame. If you start seeds early, use peat pots or pellets to avoid root disturbance.

Tips
Keep a container of parsley close to the house for easy picking. The bright foliage and compact growth habit also make parsley a good edging plant for beds and borders.

Recommended
P. crispum forms a clump of divided, bright green leaves. A biennial, it is usually grown as an annual. Cultivars may have flat or curly leaves. Flat leaves are more flavorful and curly leaves are more decorative. Dwarf cultivars are available. **Var.** *neapolitanum* (Italian parsley) has flat leaves. **Var.** *tuberosum* (Hamburg parsley) has flat leaves and large, edible roots.

P. crispum (above), *P. crispum* var. *crispum* (below)

Parsley leaves make a tasty and nutritious addition to salads. Shred freshly picked leaves and sprinkle them over your mixed greens.

Features: edible, attractive foliage
Height: 8–12" **Spread:** 12–24"
Hardiness: biennial in zones 5–8; usually grown as an annual

Rosemary
Rosmarinus

R. officinalis (below)

Growing

Rosemary prefers **full sun** but tolerates partial shade. The soil should be of **poor to average fertility** and **well drained**. Removing the woody branches encourages fresh new growth.

Tips

Where it's hardy, grow rosemary in shrub borders—or plant it in a container as a specimen. Low-growing, spreading plants can be included in rock gardens, along the tops of retaining walls or in hanging baskets.

To overwinter a container-grown plant, keep it in very light or partial shade in summer, then transfer it to a sunny window indoors, away from heat sources such as gas ranges, for winter. Keep it well watered but not soaking wet.

Rosemary's needle-like leaves are used to flavor a wide variety of culinary dishes, including chicken, pork, lamb, rice, tomato and egg dishes. Cut woody spears of rosemary to use for spearing meat chunks on the barbecue.

Recommended

R. officinalis is a dense, bushy, evergreen shrub with narrow, dark green leaves. Cultivar habits vary from strongly upright to prostrate and spreading. The winter blooms usually come in shades of blue, but pink-flowered cultivars are available. Some cultivars can survive in zone 6 in a sheltered location with winter protection. Container-grown plants rarely reach their mature size.

Rosemary can also be grown for its show of winter blossoms.

Features: fragrant, evergreen foliage; bright blue or pink flowers **Height:** 1–6'
Spread: 1–4' **Hardiness:** zone 8–10

Sweet Basil

Ocimum

The sweet, fragrant leaves of fresh sweet basil add a delicious flavor to salads and tomato-based dishes.

Growing

Sweet basil grows best in a **warm, sheltered** location in **full sun**. The soil should be **fertile, moist** and **well drained**. Pinch the tips regularly to encourage bushy growth. Plant out or direct-sow the seed after frost danger has passed in spring.

Tips

Sweet basil grows best in a warm spot outdoors, but it can be grown successfully in an indoor pot by a bright window to provide you with fresh leaves all year.

Sweet basil is a good companion plant for tomatoes—both like warm, moist growing conditions, and, when you pick tomatoes for a salad, you'll also remember to include a few sprigs of basil.

Recommended

O. basilicum is one of the most popular culinary herbs. Dozens of varieties exist, including ones with large or tiny, smooth or ruffled and green or purple leaves. Cultivars of varying height are also available.

O. basilicum 'Genovese' and 'Cinnamon' (above)
O. basilicum 'Genovese' (below)

Mix tomatoes, basil, olive oil and fresh mozzarella for a classic Tuscan delight.

Features: fragrant, decorative leaves
Height: 6–24" **Spread:** 6–24"
Hardiness: tender annual

Thyme
Thymus

T. praecox subsp. *arcticus* (above), T. x citriodorus (below)

Thyme is a popular culinary herb used in soups, stews and casseroles, and with roasts.

Growing

Thymes prefer **full sun**. The soil should be **neutral to alkaline** and of **poor to average fertility**. **Very good drainage** is essential. It is beneficial to work some leaf mold into the soil.

Tips

Thymes work well in sunny, dry locations at the front of borders, between or beside paving stones, in rock gardens, on rock walls and in containers. Creeping thyme makes a good lawn substitute for areas with reduced foot traffic. Thymes help keep the herb garden evergreen.

Recommended

T. x *citriodorus* (lemon-scented thyme) forms a mound of lemon-scented, dark green foliage with pale pink flowers. Cultivars with silver- or gold-margined leaves are available.

T. praecox subsp. *arcticus* (*T. serpyllum;* mother of thyme, creeping thyme, wild thyme) is a low-growing variety with purple flowers. Many cultivars are available. **'Elfin'** forms tiny, dense mounds of foliage. **'Lanuginosis'** (woolly thyme) is a mat-forming selection with fuzzy, gray-green leaves and pink or purple flowers.

T. vulgaris (common thyme) forms a bushy mound of dark green leaves and purple, pink or white flowers. Cultivars with variegated leaves are available.

Features: bushy habit; fragrant, decorative foliage; purple, pink or white flowers
Height: 2–12" **Spread:** 4–16"
Hardiness: zones 4–8

Autumn Fern

Dryopteris

D. erythrosora (above & below)

Autumn fern is a reliable, hardy, tough and eye-catching fern that is easy to grow.

Growing

Autumn fern grows best in **partial shade** but tolerates full sun (in consistently moist soil, with shade from the hottest afternoon sun). It also tolerates deep shade with very little loss in vigor. The soil should be **fertile, humus rich, moist** and **well drained**. Divide the plant in spring to control its spread and to propagate.

Tips

This large, impressive fern is useful as a specimen or grouped in a shaded area or a woodland garden. It is ideal for an area that stays moist but not wet, and it beautifully complements other shade-loving plants, including hostas and coral bells.

Also called: Japanese red shield fern, wood fern **Features:** decorative fronds and habit
Height: 24–36" **Spread:** 24–36"
Hardiness: zones 5–9

Recommended

D. erythrosora is an upright, evergreen perennial fern with large, slightly arching, bronzy green to dark green fronds. The new growth has a bronzy red hue. The large, red spore structures on the undersides of the fronds are conspicuous. If an extreme late frost kills the plant to the ground, it will recover and send up new growth.

Blue Lyme Grass

Leymus

L. arenarius (above), *L. arenarius* 'Blue Dune' (below)

Blue lyme grass is a tough, colorful, environmentally tolerant grass that is great for use on and near the coast.

Growing

Blue lyme grass prefers **full sun** and **moderately fertile, moist, well-drained** soil. It tolerates partial or light shade, wet or dry soil and sandy conditions. Cut back the foliage in late fall or spring. Divide in spring for fall.

Tips

Modest in clay, blue lyme grass becomes invasive in moist, loose soils. It is excellent for binding soils such as beach sand and for erosion control. The linear, blue-green leaves add wonderful contrasting color and texture to beds and borders, making it worthwhile in spite of its invasive tendencies. This grass is great for growing in containers that can be moved around to wherever an accent is needed.

Recommended

L. arenarius is an upright, perennial grass that forms clumps 24–36" tall and wide. The long, wide, arching leaves are blue-green. Its 5' spikes of blue-green flowers appear in summer and fade to tan by fall. The plant spreads by rhizomes.

Also called: sea lyme grass, European dune grass **Features:** attractive foliage and habit **Height:** 2–5' **Spread:** 24–36" to indefinite **Hardiness:** zones 4–10

Christmas Fern

Polystichum

Christmas fern is one of the lower-growing and less invasive of the hardy ferns. It is native to a large swath of the East Coast, from Canada to Florida and inland to the Mississippi River.

Growing

Christmas fern grows well in **partial to full shade**. The soil should be **fertile, humus rich** and **moist**.

Divide this fern in spring to propagate or to control its spread. Remove dead fronds and ones that look worn out in spring, before the new ones fill in.

Tips

Christmas fern can be used in beds and borders, and it is a good choice for a shaded pondside garden. It is better suited to moist rather than wet conditions. The use of the fronds as Christmas decorations gave the plant its common name. Christmas fern is mostly deer proof.

Recommended

P. acrostichoides is a vase-shaped, evergreen, perennial fern that forms a circular clump of arching, lance-shaped, dark green fronds. The fertile fronds are shorter and slightly wider than the sterile fronds.

P. acrostitchoides (above & below)

The evergreen ferns of the Polystichum *genus provide greenery year-round, and the appearance of the fronds varies significantly from species to species.*

Features: evergreen foliage; easy to grow; problem free **Height:** 12–18" **Spread:** 18–36"
Hardiness: zones 3–9

Cinnamon Fern

Osmunda

O. cinnamomea (above & below)

Ferns have a certain prehistoric mystique, and they can add a graceful elegance and textural accent to your garden.

Growing

Cinnamon ferns prefer **partial or light shade** but tolerate full sun in consistently moist soil. The soil should be **fertile, humus rich, acidic** and **moist**. Cinnamon ferns tolerate wet soil. They spread as offsets form at the plant bases.

Tips

These large ferns form an attractive mass when planted in large colonies. They can be included in beds and borders and make a welcome addition to a woodland garden or the edge of a pond.

Recommended

O. cinnamomea (cinnamon fern) has light green fronds that fan out in a circular fashion from a central point, with the whole plant resembling a badminton birdie. Produced in spring and standing straight up in the center of the plant, the leafless, bright green fertile fronds mature to cinnamon brown.

O. regalis (royal fern) forms a dense clump of foliage. The feathery, flower-like fertile fronds stand out among the sterile fronds in summer and mature to a rusty brown.

Cinnamon fern's 'flowers' are actually its conspicuous spore-producing sporangia.

Features: deciduous, perennial fern; decorative fertile fronds; attractive habit **Height:** 2–5' **Spread:** 2–4' **Hardiness:** zones 3–9

Eulalia Grass

Miscanthus

M. sinensis cultivar (above & below)

One of the most widely grown ornamental grasses available, eulalia grass offers vivid colors and ornamental plumes, with little maintenance. Of the vast array of species and cultivars to choose from, most are hardy across our state.

Growing

Eulalia grass prefers **full sun,** in **fertile, moderately moist, well-drained** soil, but it tolerates a variety of conditions.

Tips

Eulalia grass creates dramatic impact when massed in a naturalized area or mixed border, although varieties that grow quite large are best displayed as specimens. Tall varieties make effective temporary summer screens. If left alone in fall and winter, the dried foliage and showy plumes look very attractive.

Recommended

M. sinensis is a clumping, perennial grass that spreads slowly from short, thick rhizomes. The many cultivars and hybrids available offer variegated, striped or speckled foliage of one or more colors and tall, ornate, persistent plumes. '**Gracillimus**' (maiden grass) has long, fine-textured leaves. '**Morning Light**' (variegated maiden grass) is a short and delicate plant with finely white-edged leaves. '**Strictus**' (porcupine grass) is a tall, stiff, upright selection with unusual horizontal yellow bands.

Also called: Chinese silver grass, Japanese silver grass, maiden grass **Features:** colorful, decorative, strap-like foliage and showy plumes; winter interest **Height:** 3–10' **Spread:** 2–5' **Hardiness:** zones 3–8

Giant Reed Grass

Arundo

A. donax (left), *A. donax* 'Variegata' (right)

iant reed grass is an impressive specimen with many uses in the ground and when harvested. Under favorable conditions it can be invasive.

Growing

Giant reed grass grows well in **full sun, in moderately fertile, moist, well-drained** soil. Giant reed grass tolerates a variety of conditions, including wet or dry soils, sandy or clay soils and salinity. Provide **protection** from strong winds.

Giant reed grass stems are the source of reeds for musical instruments such as saxophones and clarinets.

Tips

Giant reed grass is best used as a specimen plant or at the back of a border. When cut, the stems are useful for a variety of purposes.

Recommended

A. donax is an upright, clump-forming, slightly woody, mostly evergreen grass that spreads by thick rhizomes. It has large, strap-like, arching leaves. The sturdy stems, resembling bamboo in growth, can reach 18' in height and 2" in diameter. Large, feathery spikes of light green to purple grass flowers are produced at the stem tops in mid- to late fall. **Var.** *versicolor* grows 6–8' tall and 24–36" wide, with attractive white-striped foliage.

Features: large, sturdy stems; attractive foliage, feathery flower plumes **Height:** 6–18'
Spread: 2' to indefinite
Hardiness: zones 6–10

Japanese Holly Fern
Cyrtomium falcatum

C. falcatum

apanese holly fern is a coarse-textured, heat-tolerant, easy-to-grow plant that provides a wonderful contrast to lacy-textured plants in shady spots. It can take drier conditions than many ferns and is deer resistant.

Growing

Japanese holly fern grows well in **partial to full shade**, in **fertile, moist, well-drained** soil with a lot of **organic matter** mixed in. This fern often grows best when it is not pampered. It tolerates some drought and should not be overwatered —keep the soil just moist during the growing season.

Tips

Use Japanese holly fern in shaded beds and borders, in rock gardens, at the edges of woodland gardens and in containers. Japanese holly fern also makes a great houseplant in reasonably bright rooms.

Recommended

C. falcatum is an evergreen perennial fern with slender, arching stems that grow up from erect, scaly rhizomes. It has shiny, leathery, dark green fronds with holly-like pinnae (fern leaflets). Dwarf cultivars and cultivars with variations in the foliage are available.

Features: attractive evergreen fronds; decorative habit; low maintenance
Height: 24–36" **Spread:** 24–36"
Hardiness: zones 6–10

Japanese holly fern is a great container plant indoors or out, and the attractive, long-lasting fronds can be cut for use in flower arrangements.

Northern Maidenhair Fern

Adiantum

A. pedatum (above & below)

Northern maidenhair fern is often found growing in shady, moist locations beside streams or creeks. This noninvasive plant spreads slowly and looks good planted with other shade-loving plants, such as astilbe, fringed bleeding heart, hosta, lungwort and toad lily.

Growing

This fern grows best in **partial to full shade,** in **slightly acidic, fertile, moist, well-drained** soil.

Adiantum species have been used to cure bronchitis, coughs and asthma. They are also known as good hair tonics and restoratives.

Tips

Northern maidenhair fern works best at the edge of a woodland garden. It makes a good addition to a shaded border or a shaded rock garden. This plant also does well in a streamside planting. When left to its own devices, northern maidenhair fern spreads to form colonies.

This fern is easy to propagate in fall. Just slice off a section of the thick root mass and replant in a cool spot.

Recommended

*A. **pedatum*** is an upright, deciduous plant with dark brown to black stems. It bears branched, horizontally oriented, lance-shaped fronds. The lobed, fan-shaped, medium green foliage turns yellow-green to yellow in fall. A waxy coating on the leaflets rapidly sheds water and raindrops.

Features: attractive foliage and habit; low maintenance **Height:** 12–24" **Spread:** 12–24" **Hardiness:** zones 3–8

Northern Sea Oats

Chasmanthium

This native grass is at home in moist, shady woodlands, and its bamboo-like foliage gives it a tropical flair.

Growing

Northern sea oats thrives in **full sun** or **partial shade,** although to avoid leaf scorch in full sun, the soil must stay moist; the upright, cascading habit relaxes in deep shade. The soil should be **fertile** and **moist,** but dry soils are tolerated. To deal with the vigorous self-seeding, deadhead in fall or pull the easily removed seedlings for sharing with friends or composting. Divide to control the rapid spread. Cut this plant back each spring to 2" above the ground.

Tips

Northern sea oats is a tremendous plant for moist, shady areas. Its upright to cascading habit, especially when in full bloom, is attractive alongside a stream or pond, in a large drift or in a container.

Recommended

C. latifolium forms a spreading clump of bamboo-like, bright green foliage. The scaly, dangling spikelet flowers arrange themselves nicely on delicate stems, just slightly above the foliage. The foliage sometimes turns bronze, and the flowers turn gold in fall.

C. latifolium (above & below)

The flower stalks of northern sea oats, which resemble strings of dangling fish, make interesting additions to fresh or dried arrangements.

Also called: Indian wood oats, spangle grass
Features: bamboo-like foliage; unusual flowers; winter interest **Height:** 32"–4'
Spread: 18–24" **Hardiness:** zones 5–8

Ravenna Grass

Saccharum

S. ravennae

A problem-free four-season plant, ravenna grass offers attractive spring, summer and fall foliage, fabulous plumes of flowers and a structure sturdy enough to provide interest all winter.

Growing

Grow ravenna grass in **full sun,** in **moderately fertile, well-drained** soil. Established plants tolerate drought. Excessive fertility and overwatering can cause the stems to flop over. Provide **protection** from strong winds.

Cut back the foliage and flowers in early spring to make room for new growth. Divide in spring or early summer. Deadhead the flowers if you do not want seedlings.

Much of the world's sugar supply is derived from S. officinarum (sugar cane), a close relative of ravenna grass.

Tips

Ravenna grass is an effective specimen or accent plant. Use it at the back of beds and borders, as a textured backdrop for smaller, broadleaf plants, or as a seasonal screen or hedge. The large flower spikes are used in fresh and dried arrangements.

Recommended

S. ravennae is a large, erect, clump-forming, perennial grass. It has long, arching, strap-like, gray-green foliage with white stripes. The plume-like flowers are borne on tall, stiff stems that rise well above the foliage in late summer and early fall. The foliage turns orange to bronze in fall.

Also called: plume grass, hardy pampas grass
Features: attractive foliage and habit; plume-like flowers; winter interest **Height:** 10–12'
Spread: 3–6' **Hardiness:** zones 6–10

Ribbon Grass

Phalaris

With their strikingly striped leaves, ribbon grass cultivars are among the most brightly colored grasses available.

Growing

Ribbon grass grows well in **full sun** or **partial shade**. The soil should be of **average fertility** and **moist to wet;** this grass can grow in water up to 12" deep. It can be invasive and difficult to remove once established, although less so in dry locations, so consider restricting it to a large container to control its spread.

Divide ribbon grass as needed in spring or early summer. Cut the plant back to 4" tall when it turns brown in fall.

Tips

This vigorous grass is a great addition to a moist pondside area. Ribbon grass can also be used as a groundcover or for erosion control on hard-to-maintain slopes.

Recommended

P. arundinacea **var.** *picta* is a perennial grass that spreads quickly by rhizomes. It forms clumps 18–24" tall and wide. The long, narrow, arching, green leaves have white stripes. Held above the foliage in early summer, the flowers are pale pink to white. Cultivars are available with leaves featuring bright stripes in colors such as pink, yellow, cream and green.

P. *arundinacea* var. *picta* (above)
P. *arundinacea* 'Strawberries and Cream' (below)

Planting ribbon grass in sunken containers allows you to place it in beds and borders without it taking over the garden.

Also called: gardener's garters, reed canary grass **Features:** colorful foliage
Height: 2–4' **Spread:** 36" to indefinite
Hardiness: zones 4–9

Southern Shield Fern

Thelypteris

With proper moisture, this easy-to-grow, low-maintenance native of Georgia and much of the South grows in either shade or sun.

Growing

Southern shield fern grows well in **light or partial shade**. The soil should be of **average fertility, slightly acidic, humus rich** and **moist**. Southern shield tolerates full sun when the soil is kept moist and grows adequately in hot, dry conditions, but it is most impressive in moist, shaded locations.

Divide the plants regularly or pull up extra plants to control the vigorous spread. Cut out crusty old foliage in spring, before new growth begins.

Tips

This native fern makes an attractive addition to a shaded garden or to the edge of a woodland garden. It is best used where there is plenty of room for it to spread.

Recommended

T. kunthii (*T. normalis*) is a deciduous, perennial fern that spreads by rhizomes and spores. Where it is happy, it spreads quickly. It has gently arching, large, triangle-shaped, light green fronds and white stems. The fronds are not frost hardy.

T. kunthii (above & below)

The lovely, quick-spreading southern shield fern is useful for filling lightly shaded locations.

Also called: Kunth's maiden fern, Southern wood fern, widespread maiden fern
Features: decorative foliage; fast growth; easy to maintain **Height:** 12–36"
Spread: 2–4' **Hardiness:** zones 7–10

Glossary

Acid soil: soil with a pH lower than 7.0

Annual: a plant that germinates, flowers, sets seed and dies in one growing season

Alkaline soil: soil with a pH higher than 7.0

Basal leaves: leaves that form from the crown, at the base of the plant

Bract: a modified leaf at the base of a flower or flower cluster

Corm: a bulb-like, food-storing, underground stem, resembling a bulb without scales

Crown: the part of the plant at or just below soil level where the shoots join the roots

Cultivar: a cultivated plant variety with one or more distinct differences from the species, e.g., in flower color or disease resistance

Damping off: fungal disease causing seedlings to rot at soil level and topple over

Deadhead: to remove spent flowers to maintain a neat appearance and encourage a longer blooming season

Direct sow: to sow seeds directly in the garden

Dormancy: a period of plant inactivity, usually during winter or unfavorable conditions

Double flower: a flower with an unusually large number of petals

Genus: a category of biological classification between the species and family levels; the first word in a scientific name indicates the genus

Grafting: a type of propagation in which a stem or bud of one plant is joined onto the rootstock of another plant of a closely related species

Hardy: capable of surviving unfavorable conditions, such as cold weather or frost, without protection

Hip: the fruit of a rose, containing the seeds

Humus: decomposed or decomposing organic material in the soil

Hybrid: a plant resulting from natural or human-induced cross-breeding between varieties, species or genera

Inflorescence: a flower cluster

Male clone: a plant that may or may not produce pollen but that will not produce fruit, seed or seedpods

Neutral soil: soil with a pH of 7.0

Perennial: a plant that takes three or more years to complete its life cycle

pH: a measure of acidity or alkalinity; the soil pH influences availability of nutrients for plants

Rhizome: a root-like, food-storing stem that grows horizontally at or just below soil level, from which new shoots may emerge

Rootball: the root mass and surrounding soil of a plant

Seedhead: dried, inedible fruit that contains seeds; the fruiting stage of the inflorescence

Self-seeding: reproducing by means of seeds without human assistance, so that new plants constantly replace those that die

Semi-double flower: a flower with petals in two or three rings

Single flower: a flower with a single ring of typically four or five petals

Species: the fundamental unit of biological classification; the entity from which cultivars and varieties are derived

Standard: a shrub or small tree grown with an erect main stem, accomplished either through pruning and training or by grafting the plant onto a tall, straight stock

Sucker: a shoot that comes up from the root, often some distance from the plant; it can be separated to form a new plant once it develops its own roots

Tender: incapable of surviving the climatic conditions of a given region and requiring protection from frost or cold

Tuber: the thick section of a rhizome bearing nodes and buds

Variegation: foliage that has more than one color, often patched or striped or bearing leaf margins of a different color

Variety: a naturally occurring variant of a species

Index of Recommended Species Plant Names

Entries in **bold** type indicate main plant headings.

Author Biographies

Tara Dillard enjoys gardening in Georgia's year-round gardening climate. As well as hosting her own garden show on CBS, she has worked extensively for NBC, HGTV and PBS. With degrees in engineering and horticulture, Tara has won awards for writing, speaking and designing, and she teaches at both the Atlanta Botanical Garden and Gwinnett College and for the Georgia Master Gardener Association.

Lecturing nationally, Tara takes her original concept of 'garden lifestyle design' and garden design talents on the road. As a writer, she knows that if she can help you create a beautiful garden, she can help make your entire life more beautiful. Tara Dillard has also written the books *The Garden View: Designs for Beautiful Landscapes* and *Beautiful by Design: Stunning Blueprints for Harmonious Gardens.*

Veteran garden writer **Don Williamson** is the coauthor of several popular gardening guides. He has a degree in horticultural technology and extensive experience in the design and construction of annual and perennial beds in formal landscape settings.

Acknowledgments

I thank Providence for this passion for gardening and sending along mentors to make sure I heard the call. My mentors: Louise Cofer, Bliss Page, Laura Sayers, Margaret Moseley, Mary Kistner, Richard Ludwig, Penny McHenry, Walter Reeves, Gary Peiffer, Kelvin Echols. "To each one, teach one, pass it on." *Anonymous* —*Tara Dillard*

I am blessed to work with many wonderful people, including my new and very knowledgeable friend Tara Dillard, and all the great folks at Lone Pine Publishing. I also thank The Creator.—*Don Williamson*

We thank the following people and organizations for their valuable time and beautiful images: Anne Gordon, Callaway Gardens, Stone Mountain, GA, Chris Hansen-Terra Nova Nurseries, David Cavagnaro, Dawn Loewen, Debra Knapke, Derek Fell, Horticolor, Jackson & Perkins, Janet Loughrey, Liz Klose, Lynne Harrison, Marilynn McAra, Mark Turner, Pam Beck, Peter Thompstone, Richard Hawke and the Chicago Botanic Gardens, Saxon Holt, Tim Wood, and all those who allowed us to photograph their gardens.